# SILENCE
## EQUALS CONSENT

*the sin of omission*

### Speak Now or
### Forever Lose Your Freedom!

## *William J. Federer*

American Minute Inc. • 1-888-USA-WORD • www.AmericanMinute.com

*Silence Equals Consent – The Sin of Omission:*
*Speak Now or Forever Lose Your Freedom!*

by William J. Federer

Library of Congress UNITED STATES HISTORY / RELIGION

ISBN-13: ISBN: 978-1-7369590-7-7

❧

Special thanks to Ginny Tallent, cover design and Southwest Radio Ministries (SWRC.com)

*Dedicated to*
*Pastor Rob McCoy, TPUSA FAITH*
*– a great pastor, leader, & friend*

"For if you remain silent at this time, deliverance for the Jews will arise from another place, but you and your father's family will perish. And who knows but that you have come to your royal position for such a time as this?"

– Book of Esther 4:14

❧

"Rescue those who are unjustly sentenced to death; do not stand back and let them die. Do not try to disclaim responsibility by saying you did not know about it. For God, who knows all hearts, knows yours, and he knows you knew! And He will repay everyone according to his deeds."

– Proverbs 24:11-12

❧

"If any member of the community closes their eyes when that man sacrifices one of his children to Molek … I Myself will set My face against him and his family and will cut them off from their people together."
– Leviticus 20:1-5

ঔ

"And when the blood of thy martyr Stephen was shed ... I also was standing by consenting to his death ..."
– The Apostle Paul, Acts 22:20

ঔ

"To him who knows to do good and does not do it, to him it is sin."
– James 4:17

ঔ

# CONTENTS

## COVENANT CHURCH                107

## CHURCH INFLUENCED STATE        153

# FOREWORD

It may not be by accident that you picked up this book. The fate of America and the world hangs in the balance, and you are key to turning things around. But the clock is ticking.

There are powerful truths that have been hidden for generations under religious-sounding arguments, convincing good people to be silent and let evil reign. Well-funded voices persuade citizens that it is somehow more spiritual to do nothing and let corruption spread. They teach the godly to green-light ungodly values.

Whatever happened to common sense?

This book will address some hard questions. Are you aware that just as your silence gives consent to wedding vows, it gives consent to other things? It is called "the rule of tacit admission." If you know of evil and are silent, you are an accessory to it, and will share in the judgment.

Discover the unique origins of America from a perspective you may not have considered.

For example, why in Europe was there the belief that what the king believed, his kingdom had to believe? How did the theocracy of kings convince them they were divinely appointed to force their beliefs on their subjects?

Attempts were made for centuries to limit a king's power: the Law of Freemen in St. Patrick's 5th century Senchus Mór; Alfred the Great's 9th century Doom Book; the Charter of Liberties of 1100; the Magna Carta of 1215; the English Bill of Rights of 1689.

Where did the idea come from to simply not have a king? Who were the reformers that pioneered freedom of conscience? Who proposed a plan for people to rule themselves in a "covenant" form of government? (Did you know the word "federal" is Latin for "covenant"?)

How was the ancient Hebrew Republic, pre-King Saul, the model for the Puritans?

Are you aware that Puritans who settled Massachusetts adapted their congregational church government into their civil government?

Historian James F. Cooper, Jr., explained Puritans had "local self-government, and, especially, extensive lay participation." In New England, every citizen was expected to participate in both church and state.

Have you heard of Connecticut founder Pastor Thomas Hooker, whose famous sermon in 1638 articulated the concept of "government from the consent of the governed"?

Did you know kings have "subjects" who obey but republics have "citizens" who give consent. How is Romans 13 understood differently in a self-governing republic than in a monarchy? Hint: in monarchies, subjects submit to the king; in republics, citizens ARE the king.

In a monarchy, political power flows top-down through mandates; in a republic, political power flows bottom-up through virtuous citizens voting in elections.

In contrast to Puritans who participated, were Pietists who did not participate. They emphasized a personal experience with Jesus, after which believers would be holy, withdrawing from worldly behavior, including political involvement.

How did they transition "no man can serve two masters ... God and mammon" into "God and government"?

What was the "two kingdom" concept, where believers, to be holy, were expected to choose involvement in the "sphere of the church" instead of the "sphere of government"? If spiritual people withdraw from politics, who is left to be involved but the less spiritual? How did the church's silence allow ambitious leaders to seize power and oppress the church? How did Christians in Germany allow Hitler's government to kill Jews?

How did Pietist's "withdrawal" differ from Puritan "participation," where believers were active in both church and state?

How are Puritan and Pietist theological differences of the 18th century, called the Old Light–New Light controversy, still affecting pastors and churches today?

The obvious question is: Why could it not be both — a personal experience with Jesus AND a covenant plan where citizens are involved in ruling themselves?

Should church members be negligent or should they be the salt of the earth? Is it scriptural to not care about what kind of country we are leaving to our posterity? Proverbs 13:22 states "A good man leaveth an inheritance to his children's children."

Should we just wait for Jesus to come and rescue us out of this mess? Who do you think you are going to meet when you are raptured? Jesus! Do you think Jesus loves the little children? Yes! Do you think He might wonder why you did not do anything to protect them?

Moreover, even if we can't turn the culture around, shouldn't we at least try? Jesus warned in Mark 9:42 (NLT):

> If you cause one of these little ones who trusts in me to fall into sin, it would be better for you to be thrown into the sea with a large millstone hung around your neck.

Perhaps God is giving people of faith an opportunity to show what they really believe in their hearts, through their words and actions?

History is filled with accounts of people suffering coercion and persecution by godless totalitarian governments, maligned, smeared, canceled and crushed in hopeless situations against insurmountable odds, but then, stirred by the Spirit, little nobodies rise up, small in their own eyes, but big in faith and courage, to speak truth to power and to resist evil. Isaiah 1:17 (NASB) states:

> Learn to do good; Seek justice, Rebuke the oppressor, Obtain justice for the orphan, Plead for the widow's case.

Let's believe it is possible to turn things around, and this is now our turn!

*Silence Equals Consent*

❧

# *CHRISTIAN NATIONALISM?*

# NATIONALISM IS
# THE OPPOSITE OF GLOBALISM

Why do globalists who want a one world government oppose those who wish to preserve their nation, labeling them "nationalists"?

Klaus Schwab of the World Economic Forum described the globalist goal of The Great Reset:

> You will own nothing and be happy.

This is similar to Karl Marx, who expressed in his *Communist Manifesto*:

> The theory of the communists may be summed up in the single sentence: Abolition of private property.

Jack Posobiec stated (*Human Events Daily*, OAN 11/24/22):

> The Great Reset is very much like communism … They'll tell you it is about diversity … equality … climate … But … what they want is ... total government.

People are not inclined to give up their property and freedom if everything is fine. In a crisis, though, they will panic and trade their freedom for security. The Great Reset is an orchestrated global crisis to produce dependency on international government.

Michael Rectemwald wrote in "What Is the Great Reset?" (*Imprimis*, December 2021):

> Klaus Schwab and Thierry Malleret write that if the past five centuries in Europe and America have taught us anything … it is that "acute crises contribute to boosting the power of the state."

Economist John Maynard Keynes held a similar view, writing in his book *The Economic Consequences of the Peace* (1920):

> Lenin is said to have declared "The best way to destroy the capitalist system is to debauch the currency."

Peter Thiel, founder of PayPal, in a lecture Stanford's Classical Liberalism Institute, November 18, 2022, warned not to fear world crises as much as those who promise to save us from world crises:

> The zeitgeist on the other side is "we are not going to make it for another century on this planet and therefore we need to embrace a one world totalitarian state right now" … Whatever the dangers are in the future we need to never underestimate the danger of one world totalitarian state …

> First Thessalonians 5:3, the political slogan of the antichrist is "peace and safety" … I want to suggest … we would do well to be a little more scared of the antichrist and a little a less scared

of Armageddon.

In other words, don't be afraid of the world ending, be afraid of the people who promise to save you from the world ending.

Henry L. Mencken wrote in *Notebooks*, 1956:

> The urge to save humanity is almost always only a false-face for the urge to rule it.

History is not prophetic but it is predictive. Past behavior is the best indicator of future performance. By zooming out and looking at decades, centuries, and millennia of history, it comes into focus what is going on.

# NATIONALISM DEPENDS ON THE NATION

Nationalism can be good or bad depending on the nation. In most nations, an individual's value is based on what groups you belong to. These have what is called "honor–shame" cultures:

- India's Caste System: Four major and many minor;
- Ancient Egypt's Social Classes;
- Imperial China's Hundred Family Surnames;
- Islam: Member of Ummah – male, female, dhimmi, infidel;

- European Class: royalty, peasantry;
- Communist Party Member;
- Atheistic Utilitarianism: contributing to "the state"

The latest rendition of this is intersectionality, where a person's worth is based on how many minority groups they belong to, with "trans" being superior to all others. Instead of "Christian nationalism" they are implementing a "transgender-nationalism.

Judeo-Christian Western Civilization can be summed up in a single word: "INDIVIDUAL." You have worth no matter what group you belong to. You have worth because you are made in the image of God. You are equal with everyone because God is not a respecter of persons.

President Truman stated March 6, 1946:

> Religion and democracy are founded on … the worth and dignity of the individual …

> Dictatorship … is founded on the doctrine that the individual amounts to nothing … the state is the only thing that counts.

President Eisenhower said November 9, 1954:

> Democracy is nothing in the world but spiritual conviction ... that each of us is enormously valuable because of a certain standing before our own God.

Lincoln stated in his Gettysburg Address, 1863:

> Four score and seven years ago our fathers brought forth on this continent, a new nation, conceived in liberty, and dedicated to the proposition that all men are created equal.

In America, nationalism is preserving a nation where individuals have worth regardless of what group they belong to. They have worth because they are made in the image of the Creator, who is not a respecter of persons, and therefore they are equal before the law.

The word "citizen" is Greek. It means co-sovereign, co-ruler, co-king. In America, each citizen is a co-ruler, where the government is from the consent of the governed, with the purpose of government being to guarantee to each individual their Creator–given rights.

Christians in colonial America fought to be free from a king. Kings have subjects who are "subjected" to their will. They believe they are supreme by divine right. England's James I stated:

> Kings are … God's lieutenants … upon earth … sit upon God's throne … overlord of the whole land … master over every person … having power over the life and death of every one.

Kings want absolute supremacy to rule their dominions — dominionism. Thomas Paine wrote in *Common Sense*, January 1776: "In absolute governments the king is law." France's King

Louis XIV reportedly stated: "I am the state."

Kings rule with a theocracy. King Henry VIII was not only the head of the nation of England, he was the head of the Church of England, requiring subjects to take the Oath of Supremacy, 1534:

> I declare ... that the King's Highness is the ONLY Supreme Governor of this Realm ... in all Spiritual or Ecclesiastical things.

King James I declared:

> I will make them conform themselves or I will harry them out of the land.

Christian separatist Pilgrims fled the top-down supremacy, dominionism and theocracy of a king to give birth to America's bottom-up representative republic, a covenant plan of government from the consent of the governed.

Pilgrims were non-conformists who identified with the ancient Hebrews who fled the government intimidation and persecution of Egypt's Pharaoh.

In Babylon, Jewish administrators Shadrach, Meshech and Abednigo resisted Nebuchadnezzar.

In the New Testament, Peter stood up to the Sanhedrin and chief priests in Jerusalem.

Contrary to Europe, where what the king believed the kingdom had to believe, Pennsylvania's Quaker founder William Penn said:

> Force makes hypocrites, tis persuasion only that makes converts.

Rhode Island's Baptist founder Roger Williams said:

> God requireth not a uniformity of religion to be enacted and enforced in any civil state ...

> Enforced uniformity, sooner or later, is the greatest occasion of civil war, ravishing of conscience, persecution of Christ Jesus in his servants, and of the hypocrisy and destruction of millions of souls.

Catholic founder of Maryland, Lord Baltimore gave instructions to his brother, Leonard Calvert, the governor of the expedition, 1634:

> Treat the Protestants with as much mildness and favor as justice will require.

The colony's Christian legislature advanced religious liberty with the famous Maryland Toleration Act of 1649, which stated:

> No person ... within this province ... professing to believe in Jesus Christ shall ... from henceforth be any ways troubled or molested ... in respect of his or her religion.

Where nationalism in America championed individual liberty, in socialist countries, nationalism props up totalitarian regimes where the government denies individual rights.

Socialist, communist, Islamist governments control every aspect of people's lives, as was the case in Germany with the National Socialist

Workers' Party–Nazi, or with the dictatorship of Imperial Japan.

Franklin Roosevelt condemned socialist and imperialistic nationalism, December 15, 1941:

> The German thesis that seventy or eighty million Germans were by race, training, ability, and might superior in every way to any other race in Europe – superior to about four hundred million other human beings in that area.
>
> And Japan, following suit, announced that the seventy or eighty million Japanese people were also superior to the seven or eight hundred million other inhabitants of the Orient ...
>
> Their conceit would make them masters of a region containing almost one-half the population of the earth.

Roosevelt broadcasted from the White House, Washington, D.C., December 29, 1940:

> The Nazi masters of Germany have made it clear that they intend not only to dominate all life and thought in their own country, but also to enslave the whole of Europe, and then to use the resources of Europe to dominate the rest of the world.

Roosevelt supported American nationalism, declaring, June 14, 1942:

> The belief in man, created free,

in the image of God — is the crucial difference between ourselves and the enemies we face today. In it lies the absolute unity of our alliance, opposed to the oneness of the evil we hate ...

We know that there are other millions who in their silent captivity share our belief.

We ask the German people, still dominated by their Nazi whipmasters, whether they would rather have the mechanized hell of Hitler's "New" Order or – in place of that, freedom of speech and religion, freedom from want and from fear.

We ask the Japanese people, trampled by their savage lords of slaughter, whether they would rather continue slavery and blood or – in place of them, freedom of speech and religion, freedom from want and from fear.

We ask the brave, unconquered people of the Nations the Axis invaders have dishonored and despoiled whether they would rather yield to conquerors or have freedom of speech and religion, freedom from want and from fear.

We know the answer. They know the answer. We know that man, born to freedom in the image of God, will not forever suffer the oppressors' sword.

Roosevelt continued:

The peoples of the United Nations are taking that sword from the oppressors' hands. With it, they will destroy those tyrants. The brazen tyrannies pass. Man marches forward toward the light.

I am going to close by reading you a prayer that has been written for the United Nations on this Day:

"God of the free, we pledge our hearts and lives today to the cause of all free mankind.

"Grant us victory over the tyrants who would enslave all free men and Nations.

"Grant us faith and understanding to cherish all those who fight for freedom as if they were our brothers.

"Grant us brotherhood in hope and union, not only for the space of this bitter war, but for the days to come which shall and must unite all the children of earth.

Roosevelt stated in his Four Freedoms Speech, January 6, 1941:

Voters, putting patriotism ahead of pocketbooks, will give you their applause ... to a world founded upon four essential human freedoms.

The first is freedom of speech and

expression ... The second is freedom of every person to worship God in his own way ... The third is freedom from want ... The fourth is freedom from fear ...

It is a definite basis for a kind of world attainable in our own time ... the very antithesis of the so-called new order of tyranny which the dictators seek to create with the crash of a bomb ... That new order we oppose ...

This nation has placed its destiny in the hands and heads and hearts of its millions of free men and women; and its faith in freedom under the guidance of God. Freedom means the supremacy of human rights everywhere.

On November 2, 1940, Roosevelt warned against communist nationalism subverting citizens away from American nationalism;

There are certain forces within our own national community, composed of men who call themselves American but who would destroy America. They are ... communists ... It is their constant purpose ... to weaken democracy, to destroy the free man's faith in his own cause ...

You and I ... have found the way by which men of many racial origins may live together in peace ... Americans will ... never submit to domination or influence by Nazism or Communism ...

Americans are determined to retain for themselves the right of free speech, free religion, free assembly and the right which lies at the basis of all of them — the right to choose the officers of their own Government in free elections ...

Freedom in itself is not enough. Freedom of speech is of no use to a man who has nothing to say. Freedom of worship is of no use to a man who has lost his God ...

All the forces of evil shall not prevail against it. For so it is written in the Book, and so it is written in the moral law ... It is our prayer that all lovers of freedom may join us ... unified by tolerance and by religious faith ... the spirit of peace and good will. It is the spirit of God. And in His faith is the strength of all America.

On August 16, 1945, President Harry Truman proclaimed a Day of Prayer in which he commended Americans for supporting the nation:

The warlords of Japan ... have surrendered unconditionally ... This is the end of the ... schemes of dictators to enslave the peoples of the world, destroy their civilization, and institute a new era of darkness and degradation ...

Our global victory has come from

the courage ... of free men and women united in determination to fight. It has come from the massive strength of arms ... created by peace-loving peoples who knew that unless they won, decency in the world would end.

It has come from millions of peaceful citizens ... turned soldiers overnight – who showed a ruthless enemy that they were not afraid to fight ... It has come with the help of God, Who was with us in the early days of adversity and ... Who has now brought us to this glorious day of triumph.

Let us give thanks to Him, and remember that we have now dedicated ourselves to follow in His ways.

Truman, in his Inaugural Address on January 20, 1949, contrasted between nationalism in the United States versus nationalism in communist nations. Though the United States is a republic and not a democracy, he uses the word democracy in the broad sense of people ruling themselves:

The American people stand firm in the faith which has inspired this Nation from the beginning.

We believe that all men have a right to equal justice under the law and equal opportunity to share in the common good.

We believe that all men have the right to freedom of thought and expression.

We believe that all men are created equal because they are created in the image of God. From this faith we will not be moved ...

Communism is based on the belief that man is so weak and inadequate that he is unable to govern himself, and therefore requires the rule of strong masters.

Democracy is based on the conviction that man has the moral and intellectual capacity, as well as the inalienable right, to govern himself with reason and justice.

Communism subjects the individual to arrest without lawful cause, punishment without trial, and forced labor as a chattel of the state. It decrees what information he shall receive, what art he shall produce, what leaders he shall follow, and what thoughts he shall think.

Democracy maintains that government is established for the benefit of the individual, and is charged with the responsibility of protecting the rights of the individual and his freedom in the exercise of his abilities ...

These differences between communism and democracy do not concern the United States alone. People everywhere are coming to realize that what is involved is material well-being, human dignity, and the right to believe in and worship God ...

We are aided by all who desire freedom of speech, freedom of religion, and freedom to live their own lives for useful ends ...

Steadfast in our faith in the Almighty ... we will devote our strength, our resources, and our firmness of resolve. With God's help, the future of mankind will be assured.

President Eisenhower told the American Legion Back-to-God Program, February 20, 1955:

The Founding Fathers ... recognizing God as the author of individual rights, declared that the purpose of government is to secure those rights ...

In many lands the state claims to be the author of human rights ... If the state gives rights, it can – and inevitably will – take away those rights ...

The founding fathers had to refer to the Creator in order to make their revolutionary experiment make sense ... It was because "all men are endowed by their Creator with certain inalienable rights" that men could dare to be free.

Eisenhower remarked October 24, 1954:

Atheism substitutes men for the Supreme Creator and this leads inevitably to domination and dictatorship ... It is because we believe that God intends all men to be free and equal that we demand free government.

Nationalism is a word with different meanings in different nations. In socialist nations, nationalism has been used to prop up totalitarian regimes where the state owns everything and determines everyone's destiny!

In America, "nationalism" is supporting a nation where government is from the "consent of the governed," with each citizen guaranteed God-given rights: freedom of conscience and religion, freedom to determine their own destiny!

Ronald Reagan stated in 1961:

> In this country of ours took place the greatest revolution that has ever taken place in the world's history ... The founding fathers established the idea that you and I had within ourselves the God-given right and ability to determine our own destiny.

Franklin D. Roosevelt stated on July 4, 1936:

> Patriots of 1776 ,... had broken away from indentured servitude. The source of their greatness was ... a new sense of freedom ... self-government and freedom of conscience.

# NATIONALISM USED TO BE CALLED PATRIOTISM

In America, Christian nationalism used to be called Christian patriotism. It was considered as American as football, Boy Scouts, and apple pie. In fact, past Presidents, both Democrat and Republican, encouraged it.

The word "nationalism" was not in use in America when Noah Webster compiled his *1828 American Dictionary of the English Language*. It is not in there. Yet the word "patriotism" is:

> Patriotism is the characteristic of a good citizen, the noblest passion that animates a man in the character of a citizen ...

> Love of one's country; the passion which aims to serve one's country, either in defending it from invasion, or protecting its rights and maintaining its laws and institutions in vigor and purity.

General George Washington referred to both "Christian" and "patriot" in his order to troops at Valley Forge, May 2, 1778:

> While we are zealously performing the duties of good citizens and soldiers, we certainly ought not to be inattentive to the higher duties of religion. To the distinguished character of Patriot, it should be our highest Glory to laud the

more distinguished Character of Christian.

After the Declaration of Independence was read to his troops, General Washington issued the order July 9, 1776:

> The General hopes and trusts, that every officer and man, will endeavor so to live, and act, as becomes a Christian soldier, defending the dearest rights and liberties of his country.

When Republican President Abraham Lincoln issued the Emancipation Proclamation and led the Union in freeing four million slaves, he said the words "patriotism" and "Christianity" right next to each other in his First Inaugural, March 4, 1861:

> Intelligence, patriotism, Christianity, and a firm reliance on Him who has never yet forsaken this favored land, are still competent to adjust in the best way all our present difficulty.

During the Post-Reconstruction Era, when Democrat-affiliated vigilante groups lynched blacks in the South, Republican President Theodore Roosevelt stated December 3, 1906:

> As Bishop Charles Galloway of Mississippi has said: 'The mob lynches a Negro ... Every Christian patriot in America needs to lift up his voice in loud and eternal protest against the mob spirit."

Republican President William Howard Taft had stated at a missionary conference in 1908:

> No man can study the movement of modern civilization from an impartial standpoint, and not realize that Christianity and the spread of Christianity are the basis of hope of modern civilization in the growth of popular self government.
>
> The spirit of Christianity is pure democracy. It is equality of man before God — the equality of man before the law, which is, as I understand it, the most God-like manifestation that man has been able to make.

After World War I, Democrat President Woodrow Wilson warned in his address "The Road Away from Revolution," 1923:

> We call ours a Christian civilization, a Christian conception of justice ... Our civilization cannot survive materially unless it be redeemed spiritually. It can be saved only by becoming permeated with the spirit of Christ and being made free and happy by the practices which spring out of that spirit.

At the beginning of the Great Depression, Republican President Herbert Hoover stated, October 7, 1930:

> Here less than a thousand men, inspired by the urge of freedom,

defeated a superior force intrenched in this strategic position ... This small band of patriots turned back a dangerous invasion well designed to separate and dismember the united colonies.

Democrat President Franklin D. Roosevelt stated October 6, 1935:

The 400th anniversary of the printing of the first English Bible is an event of great significance ... We trace ... the widespread dissemination of those moral and spiritual precepts that have so greatly affected the progress of Christian civilization.

Roosevelt stated May 10, 1940:

At the Pan American Conference at Buenos Aires ... we discussed ... that the Americans might have to become the guardian of Western culture, the protector of Christian civilization.

Roosevelt said at the dedication of Great Smoky Mountains National Park, September 2, 1940:

There is another enemy at home ... that ... mocks at ideals, sneers at sacrifice and pretends that the American people can live by bread alone. If the spirit of God is not in us, and if we will not prepare to give all that we have and all that we are to preserve Christian civilization in our land, we shall go to destruction.

In his D-Day Prayer, Franklin Roosevelt said:

Almighty God, our sons, the pride of our nation, this day have set upon a mighty endeavor, a struggle to preserve our republic, our religion and our civilization.

What religion was Roosevelt referring to? An Episcopalian, he wrote the prologue of a *Gideon's New Testament and Book of Psalms* that was given out by the millions to servicemen – blue ones to sailors and brown ones to soldiers. On the front page, Roosevelt wrote:

To the Armed Forces:

As Commander-in-Chief I take pleasure in commending the reading of the Bible to all who serve in the armed forces of the United States. Throughout the centuries men of many faiths and diverse origins have found in the Sacred Book words of wisdom, counsel and inspiration. It is a fountain of strength and now, as always, an aid in attaining the highest aspirations of the human soul.

Very sincerely yours – Franklin D. Roosevelt, January 25, 1941.

FDR stated May 27, 1941:

The whole world is divided between ... pagan brutality and the Christian ideal. We choose human freedom which is the Christian ideal.

FDR stated in a fireside chat, 1942:

This great war effort ... shall not

be imperiled by the handful of noisy traitors — betrayers of America, betrayers of Christianity itself.

FDR stated October 28, 1940:

We guard against the forces of anti-Christian aggression.

FDR stated November 1, 1940:

Those forces hate democracy and Christianity as two phases of the same civilization ... They oppose democracy because it is Christian. They oppose Christianity because it preaches democracy.

Roosevelt wrote August 22, 1942:

The action taken today by your Government has hastened the coming of the inevitable victory of freedom over oppression, of Christian religion over the forces of evil and darkness.

FDR stated September 1, 1941:

Preservation of these rights is vitally important ... to the whole future of Christian civilization.

Franklin Roosevelt expressed support for Christians defending the nation. Would he be labeled a "Christian nationalist" today?

Democrat President Harry S. Truman was a Christian who defended the nation at the end of World War II and the beginning of the Korean War. He proclaimed when he lit the National

Christmas Tree, December 24, 1952:

> Through Jesus Christ the world will
> yet be a better and a fairer place.

Truman said of America, August 28, 1947:

> Enduring peace can be built only
> upon Christian principles ... This is a
> Christian Nation ... As a Christian Nation
> our earnest desire is to work with men
> of good will everywhere to banish war
> ... from the world whose Creator desired
> that men of every race ... should live
> together in peace.

In 1947, during the Truman Administration,
the U.S. Corps of Cadets required:

> Attendance at chapel is part of a cadet's
> training; no cadet will be exempted. Each
> cadet will receive religious training in one
> of the three particular faiths: Protestant,
> Catholic or Jewish.

Republican President Dwight Eisenhower
defended our nation as Supreme Allied
Commander during World War II and again as
President during the Korean War. He told the
National Conference on the Spiritual Foundation
of American Democracy, November 9, 1954:

> This relationship between a spiritual
> faith ... and our form of government
> is ... obvious ... "Man is endowed by
> his Creator" ... When you come back
> to it, there is just one thing ... man is

worthwhile because he was born in the image of his God ...

Any group that ... awaken(s) all of us to these simple things ... is, in my mind, a dedicated, patriotic group that can well take the Bible in one hand and the a flag in the other, and march ahead."

Democrat President John F. Kennedy wrote to Brazil's President, Janio da Silva Quadros, January 31, 1961:

To each of us is entrusted the heavy responsibility of guiding the affairs of a democratic nation founded on Christian ideals.

Kennedy stated December 17, 1962:

Christmas ... is the most sacred and hopeful day in our civilization.

According to J. Tobin Grant's *Measuring Aggregate Religiosity in the United States*, 1952–2005, published July 30, 2008, in the year 1965, Christians made up 93 percent of America's population, consisting of 69 percent Protestant and 24 percent Catholic; with 3 percent of the population being Jewish.

Americans have always been patriotic with a Christian majority. Reminding people of this fact is not a "Christian nationalist" plot to return to a former era, but by the same token, it is the height of ungratefulness for non-Christians to benefit from tolerance granted them by Christians only to turn around and be intolerant of Christians.

∽

## LEADERS ENCOURAGED CHRISTIANITY AND PATRIOTISM

Other famous Americans who encouraged both Christianity and patriotism included Rev. John Witherspoon, a signer of the Declaration, who told his Princeton students, May 17, 1776:

> He is the best friend to American liberty, who is most sincere and active in promoting true and undefiled religion ... It is in the man of piety and inward principle, that we may expect to find the uncorrupted patriot ... God grant that in America true religion and civil liberty may be inseparable.

Dr. Benjamin Rush, a signer of the Declaration of Independence, explained in *Essays, Literary, Moral, and Philosophical*, 1798:

> The only means of establishing and perpetuating our republican forms of government ... is ... the universal education of our youth in the principles of Christianity by the means of the Bible.

Daniel Webster stated at the Bicentennial Celebration of the landing of the Pilgrims at

Plymouth Rock, December 22, 1820:

> Whatever makes men good Christians, makes them good citizens.

Supreme Court Justice Joseph Story, appointed by President James Madison, was Harvard's first Dane Professor of Law. He stated in a speech at Harvard in 1829:

> There never has been a period of history, in which the Common Law did not recognize Christianity as lying at its foundation.

In 1833, Justice Story wrote that in America:

> Government can not long exist without an alliance with religion; and that Christianity is indispensable to the true interests and solid foundations of free government.

The New York Legislature stated in 1838:

> Our Government depends for its being on the virtue of the people, – on that virtue that has its foundation in the morality of the Christian religion; and that religion is the common and prevailing faith of the people.

Clara Barton, founder of the American Red Cross, stated of the wounded Civil War soldiers:

> What could I do but go with them, or work for them and my country? The patriot blood of my father was warm in my veins.

*The New York Times,* November 18, 1992, printed Mississippi Governor Kirk Fordice's statement:

> The less we emphasize the Christian religion the further we fall into the abyss of poor character and chaos in the United States of America.

Patricia U. Bonomi, professor emeritus of New York University, wrote in "Religious Pluralism in the Middle Colonies" (Divining America, TeacherServe, National Humanities Center, accessed 7/23/23):

> The colonists were about 98 percent Protestant.

DELAWARE, the first state to ratify the U.S. Constitution, stated in its 1776 State Constitution:

> Every person ... appointed to any office ... shall ... subscribe ... "I ... profess faith in GOD THE FATHER, and in JESUS CHRIST His only Son, and in the HOLY GHOST, one God, blessed for evermore; and I do acknowledge the Holy Scriptures of the Old and New Testament to be given by Divine inspiration."

PENNSYLVANIA, the second state to ratify the U.S. Constitution, stated in its 1776 State Constitution, signed by Ben Franklin:

> Each member, before he takes his seat, shall ... subscribe ... "I do believe

in one GOD, the Creator and Governor of the Universe, the Rewarder of the good and the Punisher of the wicked. And I do acknowledge the Scriptures of the Old and New Testament to be given by Divine Inspiration."

NEW JERSEY, the third state to ratify the U.S. Constitution, stated in its 1776 State Constitution:

All persons, professing a belief in the faith of any PROTESTANT sect, who shall demean themselves peaceably under the government ... shall be capable of being elected.

GEORGIA, the fourth state to ratify the U.S. Constitution, stated in its 1777 State Constitution:

Representatives shall be chosen out of the residents in each county ... and they shall be of the PROTESTANT religion.

CONNECTICUT, the fifth state to ratify the U.S. Constitution, retained its 1662 Colonial Constitution, which was established PROTESTANT CONGREGATIONAL till 1818:

By the Providence of GOD ... having from their ancestors derived a free and excellent constitution ... whereby the legislature depends on the free and annual election ... The free fruition of such liberties and privileges as humanity, civility and CHRISTIANITY call for.

MASSACHUSETTS, the sixth state to ratify the U.S. Constitution, stated in its 1780 State Constitution, written by John Adams:

> Any person ... before he ... execute the duties of his ... office ... [shall] subscribe ... "I ... declare, that I believe the CHRISTIAN religion, and have a firm persuasion of its truth" ... The legislature shall ... authorize the support and maintenance of public PROTESTANT teachers of piety, religion and morality.

MARYLAND, the seventh state to ratify the U.S. Constitution, stated in its 1776 State Constitution:

> No other test ... ought to be required, on admission to any office ... than such oath of support and fidelity to this State ... and a declaration of a belief in the CHRISTIAN religion.

SOUTH CAROLINA, the eighth state to ratify the U.S. Constitution, stated in its 1778 State Constitution:

> No person shall be eligible to a seat ... unless he be of the PROTESTANT religion ... The CHRISTIAN PROTESTANT religion shall be deemed ... the established religion of this State.

NEW HAMPSHIRE, the ninth state to ratify

the U.S. Constitution, stated in its 1784 State Constitution:

> No person shall be capable of being elected ... who is not of the PROTESTANT religion.

VIRGINIA, the tenth state to ratify the U.S. Constitution, stated in its 1776 State Constitution, Bill of Rights, written with the help of James Madison and George Mason:

> It is the mutual duty of all to practice CHRISTIAN forbearance, love, and charity towards each other.

NEW YORK, the eleventh state to ratify the U.S. Constitution, stated in its 1777 State Constitution:

> The United American States ... declare ... "Laws of nature and of NATURE'S GOD ... All men are created equal; that they are endowed by their CREATOR with certain unalienable rights ... Appealing to the SUPREME JUDGE of the world ... A firm reliance on the protection of DIVINE PROVIDENCE" ... The People of this State, ordain ... the free exercise and enjoyment of religious profession and worship, without discrimination ... Provided, That the liberty of conscience, hereby granted, shall not be so construed as to excuse acts of licentiousness [sexuality immorality]."

NORTH CAROLINA, the twelfth state to ratify the U.S. Constitution, stated in its 1776 State Constitution:

> No person, who shall deny the being of GOD or the truth of the PROTESTANT religion, or the Divine authority either of the Old or New Testaments, or who shall hold religious principles incompatible with the freedom and safety of the State, shall be capable of holding ... office.

RHODE ISLAND, the thirteenth state to ratify the U.S. Constitution, retained its 1663 Colonial Constitution till 1843, which stated:

> By the blessing of God ... a full liberty in religious concernements ... rightly grounded upon GOSPEL principles, will give the best and greatest security ... in the true CHRISTIAN faith and worship of God ... They may ... defend themselves, in their just rights and liberties against all the enemies of the CHRISTIAN faith.

Catholics were initially allowed only in Maryland, Pennsylvania, and to a degree in New York. Bishop John Carroll wrote to Rome, 1790:

> The thirteen provinces of North America rejected the yoke of England, they proclaimed, at the same time, freedom of conscience ... Before this great event, the CATHOLIC faith

had penetrated two provinces only, Maryland and Pennsylvania. In all the others the laws against CATHOLICS were in force.

President Washington wrote to Catholic Bishop John Carroll, March 1790:

> Your fellow citizens will not forget the patriotic part which you took in the accomplishment of their Revolution ... May the members of your society in America, animated alone by the pure spirit of Christianity ... enjoy every temporal and spiritual felicity.

After the terrorist attacks on the Pentagon and Twin Towers in New York, *Newsweek* published its September 24, 2001, issue with the cover "After the Terror – God Bless America."

On December 23, 2021, Jeffrey M. Jones of Gallup.com published the report "How Religious Are Americans?" (*The Short Answer*):

> According to an average of all 2021 Gallup polling, about three in four Americans said they identify with a specific religious faith. By far the largest proportion, 69%, identify with a Christian religion, including 35% who are Protestant, 22% Catholic and 12% who identify with another Christian religion or simply as a "Christian."

Tolerance evolved from Pilgrims and Puritans

to all Protestants and Catholics, to Jews, liberal pseudo–Christian groups, Monotheists and Polytheists, to all religions, including Atheists, Islamists, and Satanists. Ironically, the last ones in want to kick the first ones out. They are intolerant of the beliefs that extended tolerance to them.

Ronald Reagan stated August 23, 1984:

> The frustrating thing is that those who are attacking religion claim they are doing it in the name of tolerance. Question: Isn't the real truth that they are intolerant of religion?

# PROJECTION

Why does the mainstream media insist on calling Christian patriots "Christian nationalists"? For the same reason they call Pro-Life supporters "anti-abortion." Negative word association. They want to malign them with the negative word "anti" in order to sway public opinion against them.

No Pro-Life group labels itself "anti-abortion." Yet every mainstream new article that covers the subject labels Pro-Life people "anti-abortion."

In the same way, globalists want to malign Bible-believing Christians and traditional

*Silence Equals Consent*

Catholics who love their country by using the negative-sounding label "Christian nationalist."

Bob Unruh wrote in *WND.com*, April 1, 2024:

> State ... attacks Christians with a so-called "non-discrimination" agenda that actually discriminates against people of faith.

When one understands Cold War "color revolution" tactics, their game plan is clear:

> 1. Label political opponents who hold traditional values as "Nationalists";
>
> 2. Have FBI dress up as "Nationalists" and commit terrorist attacks;
>
> 3. Use that as an excuse to carry out J6–style arrests those with traditional values, Pro-Life Catholics and Bible-believing Christians, eliminating political opposition.

*Washington Times* reported January 30, 2024, "Six Pro-Lifers Convicted: Possible 10 Year Sentence for Nashville Rescue."

What is happening is called psychological projection. The intolerant activists accuse Christians of being intolerant, when in reality, it is they who are intolerant of Christians. It is the narcissistic response of a guilty person, to avoid being caught, accusing the innocent person of what they, themselves, are guilty of.

It is called blame–shifting, where the attacker blames the victim. Little children instinctively do this, saying things like, "I did not start the fight – you did!" A cheating spouse will accuse the faithful spouse of being unfaithful.

In the Bible, Potiphar's wife accused Joseph of lusting after her when she was lusting after him. Nero is attributed with setting fire to Rome, yet he blamed it on Christians.

Agenda-driven activists engage in "fear mongering," trying to spread panic that Christians want to "seize power" and "force" their beliefs on others, when in reality, it is they who are seizing power and forcing LGBTQ, Trans, Drag Queen story hour beliefs on the children of Christians.

Nancy Pelosi called it the "wrap–up smear":

> It's a diversionary tactic ... You demonize and then – the 'wrap–up smear' ... You smear somebody with falsehoods ... and then ... it's reported in the press.

Harry Reid accused Mitt Romney of not paying his taxes, causing negative press which cost him the election. *Time* magazine fact checked that Romney did pay his taxes. When they questioned Reid, he responded, "I lied about Romney, but he didn't win, did he?"

Political advisor David Axelrod stated on National Public Radio, April 19, 2010:

> In Chicago, there was an old tradition of throwing a brick through your own campaign office window, and then

calling a press conference to say that you've been attacked.

*The New York Times* reported "Cash Flowed to Clinton Foundation Amid Russian Uranium Deal: Hillary Clinton approved Russian Uranium deal after $2 million donated to Clinton Foundation." This resulted in President Trump being spied upon and having to go through an impeachment trial. When what Hillary had done became known, all she had to do was pay a fine.

*TheGatewayPundit.com* reported: "Hillary Clinton campaign pays $113,000 FEC fine in admission of guilt for producing Steele Dossier."

Biden admitted on C-SPAN to extorting Ukraine, saying he told Ukraine officials to stop investigating his son or he would hold back billions of U.S. aid. When this became known, his backers accused Trump of extorting Ukraine, resulting in another impeachment trial.

When inside sources realized that Biden illegally had classified documents in his garage next to his Corvette, his FBI staged a very visible raid on Trump's Mar-a-Lago Club so the headlines would accuse Trump of what Biden was guilty of, allowing Biden to get a pass.

In the same way, agenda-driven activists are blaming Christians for what they are guilty of. They are the ones setting up a type of irreligious nationalism; a satanist theocracy; a trans-dominionism, using Critical Race Theory, DEI, ESG, to censor and cancel Bible–believing Christians and Pro-Life Catholics.

Their anti-Christian nationalism denies freedom of conscience and freedom of speech, censors and cancels people who do not agree with them, causing them to lose their jobs, and even subject them to pre-dawn FBI raids, J6–style arrests, and Soviet-era prison sentences.

# BOOGEYMAN DU JOUR

Globalists attempt to paint opponents as enemies of democracy, while they "seize the moral high ground" and "virtue signal," by presenting themselves as caring about democracy when all they really want is power.

In George Orwell's novel, *Nineteen Eighty–Four,* the character O'Brien explained to Winston:

> "There is no way in which the Party can be overthrown. The rule of the Party is forever. Make that the starting-point of your thoughts ... The Party maintains itself in power. Now tell me why we cling to power. What is our motive? Why should we want power? Go on, speak,"

Winston said feebly,

"You are ruling over us for our own good ... You believe that human beings are not fit to govern themselves, and therefore –"

"That was stupid, Winston, stupid!" O'Brien said.

"You should know better than to say a thing like that ... I will tell you the answer to my question ... The Party seeks power entirely for its own sake. We are not interested in the good of others; we are interested solely in power ... pure power ... We are different from all the oligarchies of the past ...

German Nazis and the Russian Communists came very close to us in their methods, but they never had the courage to recognize their own motives.

They pretended, perhaps they even believed, that they had seized power unwillingly and for a limited time, and that just round the corner there lay a paradise where human beings would be free and equal.

We are not like that. We know that no one ever seizes power with the intention of relinquishing it. Power is not a means, it is an end. One does not establish a dictatorship in order to safeguard a revolution; one makes the revolution in order to establish the dictatorship ... The object of power is power. Now do you begin to understand me?"

David Horowitz wrote in *Rules for the Revolution–The Alinsky Model* (Freedom Center, 2009, p. 8–9):

> *The New Republic's* Ryan Lizza nicely illustrates ... When Alinsky would ask new students why they wanted to organize, they would invariably respond with selfless bromides about wanting to help others. Alinsky would then scream back at them that there was a one-word answer: "You want to organize for POWER!"

World War I Fighter Ace Eddie Rickenbacker warned:

> Every time the liberals discover ... a new way to circumvent the constitutional limits of the Federal power, they pile up more power in Washington at the expense of individual liberty across the land ...

> The liberal would sweep aside the constitutional restraints upon government in a blind rush to supply food, clothes, houses and financial security from birth to death, from the cradle to the grave for everybody ...

> The conservative knows that to regard man of a part of an undifferentiated mass is to consign him to ultimate slavery ... Government is like fire: a dangerous servant and a fearful master ... [It needs] limits.

Rickenbacker warned in "Americanism versus

Communism," November 1, 1971:

> A government that is large enough to give you all you want is large enough to take all you own first.

President Gerald Ford stated October 19, 1974:

> What they don't tell us when they propose all these benefits that they are going to give you from our government ... that a government big enough to give us everything we want is a government big enough to take from us everything we have.

In 1918, Mencken explained how politics needs an enemy to get people to panic:

> The whole aim of practical politics is to keep the populace alarmed - and hence clamorous to be led to safety - by menacing it with an endless series of hobgoblins, all of them imaginary.

*The Telegraph,* December 12, 2023, highlighted this maligning in an article on Hollywood producer, "Rob Reiner is deluded about 'Christian nationalism'—The *God and Country* trailer presents ordinary religious Americans as nationalist boogeymen":

> The outspoken Democrat announced that 'God and Country,' a documentary about the left's boogeyman du jour, will be hitting the theaters ...
>
> Reiner's ... examples of Christian Nationalism ... are so broad that even

the late Queen Elizabeth had a brush with it ... (and) ... Billy Graham ...

The inescapable conclusion is that average Christian beliefs and average Christian engagement in the public sphere is exactly what Reiner and his abettos [collaborators] hope to target. They want to shame followers of Jesus from taking part in the very same political activities their secular counterparts do.

*TheGatewayPundit.com* published February 17, 2024: "Atheist Rob Reiner Goes on MSNBC and Explains How He Understands Christianity Better Than Christians."

*Breitbart.com* published February 20, 2024: "Nolte: Like All Rob Reiner Movies, *God And Country* Flops With $38K Opening":

In 85 theaters, Reiner's bigoted attack on Christians who dared to vote for Donald Trump earned just $38,415 over four days ... which is incredibly low ... Reiner and *The New York Times* believe Christian ideas should be automatically disqualified for being Christian.

After a month, the headline ran March 10, 2024: "Nolte: Rob Reiner's Fascist 'God & Country' Doc Grosses Pathetic $60K Worldwide."

# RIGHTS FROM GOD,
# NOT GOVERNMENT

*TheGatewayPundit.com* reported February 23, 2024, "Politico Reporter on MSNBC Frets That Christian Nationalists Believe Americans' Rights Come From God, Not the Government":

> Heidi Przybyla, a reporter for Politico, appeared on MSNBC this week and fretted as she explained that Christian Nationalists believe that Americans' rights are granted by God and not Congress or the Supreme Court.
>
> Leaving aside her ridiculous distinctions between Christian Nationalists and other Christians, the rights of Americans DO come from God and not the government, which anyone knows if they have read the country's founding documents.
>
> How is this person even allowed to comment on politics on TV with this level of dishonesty or stupidity? This is a perfect example of why trust in the media is in the gutter.

The satire site *BabylonBee.com* published February 23, 2024, "Get A Load Of These Insane Christian Nationalists Who Believed Rights Come From God And Not The Government":

> You're not gonna believe this.

Check out this list of radical Christian nationalists who believe inalienable human rights are endowed on them by some sort of higher power, a Creator, or something like that, and not by the federal government.

1. This idiot named John Locke. This loser thought liberty came from the Law of Nature ...

2. Total loser Thomas Jefferson. Just look at the unhinged insanity in the eyes of this deranged radical.

3. This stupid thing called The Declaration of Independence. "We hold these truths to be self-evident, that all men are created equal, that they are endowed by their Creator with certain unalienable Rights..." UHG. Who wrote this #!?@?

4. Some dummy named Thomas Paine. Paine claimed that every child born into the world must be considered as deriving its existence from God. Uh, yeah. Ok, weirdo.

5. Moron and inventor of lightning Benjamin Franklin. This creep said that liberty is derived from the laws of God. Put this one on an FBI Watchlist…he's about to storm the Capitol.

These guys are all dummies. Do human rights come from God? Never.

Rights come from the government and are disseminated to the population through the mainstream media. We need to stamp out this ridiculous scourge of Christian nationalism wherever we see it ... before we lose our democracy.

*TheGatewayPundit.com* published Mike LaChance's article, February 29, 2024 "Christian Groups Demand Apology From Politico Over Reporter's Stupid Comments About American Rights and Christian Nationalism":

> Last week, a reporter for the liberal outlet *Politico* appeared on MSNBC and suggested that if you're an American who believes that your rights come from God and not the government, that you're a Christian Nationalist.

> This was meant to insult all Christians, conservatives, Trump supporters, and all of the other people who are despised by the left. Now at least two Christian groups are calling out *Politico* and demanding an apology ...

> *Politico* is facing formal calls for an apology from two of America's leading faith-focused organizations: the Family Research Council and Catholic Vote.

> FRC President Tony Perkins and Catholic Vote President Brian Burch fired off a letter Wednesday to Politico's Editor-in-Chief John Harris, *Politico*

CEO Goli Sheikholeslami, and Jan Brewer, the Deputy CEO of Politico's parent Axel Springer, demanding an apology for Przybyla's attack on Christians.

Saying Przybyla "demonstrated a disqualifying lack of knowledge of the United States of America's founding documents and a prejudicial view toward American religious groups" ...

Politico's reporter failed to acknowledge "that our own Republic was founded on the belief that our rights come from God, not earthly kings or government," a revolutionary idea "clearly articulated in the Declaration of Independence."

"Ms. Przybyla is charged with reporting accurately ... It is deeply disturbing, therefore, that she appeared unaware of the opening of the Declaration of Independence or to its references of 'the Laws of Nature and of Nature's God' ...

Perkins and Burch called out Przybyla for "an attempt to spread misinformation about Christians by creating the perception that they hold unique beliefs that pose a distinct and, in her words 'extremist,' threat to our country."

Phyllis Schlafly Eagles reported March 1, 2024:

Earlier this week, Heidi Przybyla co-authored a *Politico* article warning about the dangers of so-called "Christian Nationalism" in the Trump world.

She proceeded to go on MSNBC to discuss it. She said that the thing that distinguishes Christian Nationalists from other Christians is that Christian Nationalists believe "our rights as Americans ... come from God," and that makes them dangerous.

The keen observer may notice that she is almost exactly quoting the Declaration of Independence. Heidi isn't railing against "Christian Nationalism," she's railing against the American Founding.

@WadeMiller_USMC posted:

@MSNBC helpfully makes it clear their disdain for Christians in America. She says that if you believe that your rights come from God, you aren't a Christian, you are a Christian nationalist.

Somehow they seem to not mention that our own founding documents make this proclamation, as have most Americans throughout our history.

The radical Atheist Globalists are coming to try to crush ordinary American citizens.

The same globalists that fund teaching Christians *not* to get involved politically are funding activists *to get them involved* politically. Megan Basham wrote in *First Things*, January 22, 2024, "Follow the Money to the After Party":

> Rockefeller's bankrolling of After Party Bible studies is a red flag. In the same grant round … is a group seeking to promote the "leadership of rural LGBTQ+ people.

It is a brilliant strategy, motivate supporters while demotivating opponents, shaming them into inactivity by labeling them "Christian nationalists."

Hillary Clinton condescendingly described her opponents "clinging to their guns and their Bibles." She inadvertently described our first President, George Washington, who warned in his Farewell Address, September 19, 1796:

> Religion and Morality are indispensable supports. In vain would that man claim the tribute of Patriotism, who should labor to subvert these great pillars of human happiness ...

> Real Patriots, who may resist the intrigues ... are liable to become suspected and odious; while its tools and dupes usurp the applause and confidence of the people, to surrender their interests.

Contrary to accusations of dominionism, racial supremacy, or theocracy, patriots believe "all men are created equal, that they are endowed by their

Creator with certain unalienable rights ... that to secure these rights, governments are instituted among men, deriving their just powers from the consent of the governed."

Patriots believe citizens should have freedom of conscience, religion, speech, press, assembly, self-defense, a fair and speedy trial by a jury of peers, with no cruel and unusual punishment.

# HOW CAN YOU FORCE FREEDOM

Mainstream media calls Christian patriots "Christian Nationalists" and accuse them of wanting to "force" their beliefs on others, but how can you force freedom on someone?

Patriots do not want to force their beliefs on others, they simply do not want an all-powerful government forcing its beliefs on them. They do not want government legislating immorality. Patriots simply seek to preserve the same individual freedoms the founders sought.

Like the founding fathers, patriots want to defend freedoms for the sake of future generations.

Instead of "dominionism," patriots want "freedomism." How can it be bad to want to guarantee to people their individual freedoms?

If corporate media told the truth, it would

disrupt their narrative. How would it scare viewers? Imagine the warning, "Christian Nationalists want to force people to have freedom of religion, freedom of conscience, freedom of speech, freedom of press, freedom of assembly. How dangerous!"

Patriots desire to guarantee to both Christians and non-Christians the freedoms upon which this country was founded.

How could people be afraid of Christians wanting to follow the leadership example of Jesus who said in Matthew 20:25-28:

> You know that the rulers of the Gentiles lord it over them, and those who are great exercise authority over them. Yet it shall not be so among you; but whoever desires to become great among you, let him be your servant.
>
> And whoever desires to be first among you, let him be your slave— just as the Son of Man did not come to be served, but to serve, and to give His life a ransom for many.

What do people have to fear if genuine Christians are in leadership? Servants? Public servants! The same public servants that founded this country and gave them the freedoms they now enjoy, the freedoms they are unfortunately twisting to banish Christians from leadership.

*Silence Equals Consent*

❧

# *FREEDOM OF CONSCIENCE*

❦

# SIX VARIABLES

In the examination of where the concept of Christians being silent came from, there are six variables throughout history that must be examined: church, state, king, people, top-down, bottom-up.

These six variables have interacted differently over the centuries, with each change costing thousands of lives:

> *church and state ruled *top-down* by same king in different roles;

> *church ruled *top-down* by popes and bishops, and state ruled *top-down* by kings;

> *church governed *bottom-up* by people, and state governed *top-down* by kings;

> *church and state governed *bottom-up* by the same people in different roles.

The same person can have different roles, for example a spouse can also be a parent. A citizen can have a role in the church and a role in the state.

Then the progression went in reverse as the Pietist movement convinced spiritual people to withdraw from their role in politics, leaving the less spiritual, ambitious politicians to seize power.

> *church and state governed *bottom-up*

by same people in different roles

 *church governed *bottom-up* by "holy" people, and state governed *bottom-up* by the less holy, ambitious politicians;

 *church governed *bottom-up* by "holy" people and state ruled *top-down* by ambitious politicians;

 *church and state ruled *top-down* by same ambitious politicians.

The progression of these variables through history will be explained in the following chapters.

# DEFAULT SETTING FOR GOVERNMENT IS GANGS

The default setting for human government is gangs. If all laws and police were gone tomorrow, what would happen? Things would be fine for a few days, but then gangs would start robbing stores.

When word got out that no one stopped them, there would be a mad rush and the stores would be emptied. Then mobs of squatters would start going house to house. The most ruthless and criminal would become the bad gang leader.

You would want to organize your neighborhood for defense. One of your neighbors might know better how to fight and everyone would tell him:

you be our captain – our good gang leader.

Before you know it, we are back to a gang structure, with good gang leaders protecting us from bad gang leaders.

You would have to pick sides, which gang to belong to, and that gang leader would demand loyalty in exchange for risking himself for your protection or for your portion of the booty.

A glorified gang leader is called a king. This is the most common form of government in world history. Gang leaders use fear to make people obey. Machiavelli gave his diabolical advice:

> Since it is difficult to join them together, it is safer to be feared than to be loved ... Men shrink less from offending one who inspires love than one who inspires fear.

During the Revolutionary War, Thomas Paine wrote in his third edition of *Common Sense*, published in Philadelphia, February 14, 1776:

> The present race of kings ... could we take off the dark covering of antiquity, and trace them to their first rise, that we should find the first of them nothing better than the principal ruffian of some restless gang, whose savage manners or preeminence in subtility obtained him the title of chief among plunderers; and who by increasing in power, and extending his depredations, over-awed the quiet and

defenseless to purchase their safety.

Power, like gravity, always wants to concentrate into the hands of one person. A gang leader with enough power is called by a different name: pharaoh, caesar, tsar, kaiser, khan, tyrant, dictator, emperor, comrade, premier, chief or king.

From the beginning of recorded history, concentrated power is the norm: Nimrod of the Tower of Babel, Gilgamesh of Uruk, Pharaoh Ramesses of Egypt, Sennacharib of Assyria, Nebuchadnezzar of Babylon, Cyrus of Persia, Alexander the Great of Macedonia, Julius Caesar of Rome, Attila the Hun, Maharajah Chandragupta of India, Ottoman Sultan Suleiman, Mongolian Genghis Khan, Aztec Montezuma, Russian Tsar Ivan the Terrible, German Kaiser Wilhelm, El Jefe Fidel Castro, and El Presidente.

As the centuries went on, the kingdoms got bigger, because with military advancements kings could kill more people. Instead of Cain killing Abel with a rock, they could kill with bronze weapons, iron weapons, phalanx spears, composite recurve bows, scimitar swords, gunpowder, and more. The weapon improved but fallen human nature stays the same.

With technological advancements kings could track more people. Around 3 B.C., Augustus Caesar implemented a worldwide tracking system – "that the whole world should be enrolled." A census counting millions of people was modern technology back then. If Augustus could have had access to cell phones, 5G, cameras, facial recognition and satellites, he probably would have been tempted to use those to track people.

Wherever there is a king, it is a hierarchical system. If you are friends with the king, you are more equal. If you are not friends with the king, you are less equal. If you are an enemy of the king, you are dead – it is called treason – or you are a slave.

Some might think slavery started in 1619. No, wherever you had the first king on top, you had slaves on the bottom. Kings considered it an act of mercy to not kill you after defeating you in battle.

Finally, the King of England had the biggest kingdom on planet Earth. The sun never set on the British Empire. He was a globalist, a one world government guy, with him at the top.

Anybody who can plot on a graph can predict the trajectory that at some point this is going to max out on a global level as foretold in the Book of Revelation. Jesus said, the wheat and tares grow together until the harvest (Matthew 13:30).

What is rare in world history is people finding a way to rule themselves without a king.

# GLOBALISM BEGAN AT THE TOWER OF BABEL

The first attempt at a one world government was Nimrod. He ruled top-down, wanting people to fear him rather than God, dictating both political and religious views. He is reputed for having built the Tower of Babel.

Genesis 10:8-10: "Cush begat Nimrod: he began to be a mighty one in the earth ... and the beginning of his kingdom was Babel."

Genesis 11:1-9 (NIV) explained further:

> Now the whole world had one language and a common speech. As people moved eastward, they found a plain in Shinar and settled there.

> They said to each other, "Come, let's make bricks and bake them thoroughly." They used brick instead of stone, and tar for mortar. Then they said, "Come, let us build ourselves a city, with a tower that reaches to the heavens, so that we may make a name for ourselves; otherwise we will be scattered over the face of the whole earth."

> But the Lord came down to see the city and the tower the people were building. The Lord said, "If as one people speaking the same language they have begun to do this, then nothing they

plan to do will be impossible for them. Come, let us go down and confuse their language so they will not understand each other."

Josephus wrote in chapter 4 of *Antiquities of the Jews*, 94 A.D.:

Now the sons of Noah were three, – Shem, Japheth, and Ham, born one hundred years before the Deluge. These first of all descended from the mountains into the plains, and fixed their habitation there ... The plain in which they first dwelt was called Shinar.

God also commanded them to send colonies abroad, for the thorough peopling of the earth, that they ... might cultivate a great part of the earth, and enjoy its fruits after a plentiful manner. But they ... did not obey God ...

God admonished them again to send out colonies; but they, imagining the prosperity they enjoyed was not derived from the favor of God, but supposing that their own power was the proper cause of the plentiful condition they were in, did not obey him ...

They added to this their disobedience to the Divine will, the suspicion that they were therefore ordered to send out separate colonies, that, being divided asunder, they might the more easily be oppressed.

*Silence Equals Consent*

Now it was Nimrod who excited them to such an affront and contempt of God. He was the grandson of Ham, the son of Noah, a bold man, and of great strength of hand. He persuaded them not to ascribe it to God, as if it was through his means they were happy, but to believe that it was their own courage which procured that happiness.

He also gradually changed the government into tyranny, seeing no other way of turning men from the fear of God, but to bring them into a constant dependence on his power.

He also said he would be revenged on God, if he should have a mind to drown the world again; for that he would build a tower too high for the waters to be able to reach ...

Now the multitude were very ready to follow the determination of Nimrod, and to esteem it a piece of cowardice to submit to God; and they built a tower, neither sparing any pains, nor being in any degree negligent about the work: and, by reason of the multitude of hands employed in it, it grew very high, sooner than any one could expect; but the thickness of it was so great, and it was so strongly built, that thereby its great height seemed, upon the view, to be less than it really was.

It was built of burnt brick, cemented together with mortar, made of bitumen, that it might not be liable to admit water.

When God saw that they acted so madly, he did not resolve to destroy them utterly, since they were not grown wiser by the destruction of the former sinners; but he caused a tumult among them, by producing in them diverse languages, and causing that, through the multitude of those languages, they should not be able to understand one another.

The place wherein they built the tower is now called Babylon, because of the confusion of that language which they readily understood before.

Nimrod's Tower of Babel was the first attempt at a "world government." God confused the languages and the people scattered into language groups that turned into nations. Nations, therefore, were God's invention to postpone a one-world government. Nations would complete and cancel out each other's ambitions, hindering one person from uniting the world in a defiant, oppressive manner as Nimrod did.

Unfortunately, every generation has some Nimrod-like king who arises wanting to conquer other nations, and if left unchecked by dying, any one of them would have been happy to continue conquering till they ruled the world.

God is in favor of nations. He told Abraham "thou shalt be a father of many nations" (Genesis 17:4).

Nations have borders. Before Moses took the Israelites into the Promised Land, he told Moses what the borders of Israel would be. He instructed Israelites to respect the borders of Edom and not cross them (Exodus 25; Numbers 21).

Paul spoke in Athens, Acts 17:26: "God hath made of one blood all nations of men who dwell on the face of the earth, and hath determined ... the bounds of their habitation."

Nations were God's way of taking the Tower of Babel and scattering it; taking a one-world government and separating it. The self-interests of each nation would be a check on the other nations.

In a similar way the U.S. Constitution took the power of a king and separated it into three branches, with each being a check on the others, and then separating power from Federal to state level. The Constitution, at its most basic level, is a way to prevent one-person rule, preventing a President from ruling through mandates and executive orders.

# CHURCH BORN INTO PERSECUTION

The Church was born into a one-world anti-

Christian government — The Roman Empire.

After Christ's resurrection and the disciples receiving the Holy Spirit, the Church was immediately persecuted. Eleven of the twelve Apostles were martyred. For the next three centuries there were ten major persecutions:

Josh McDowell and his son Sean explained in *Evidence That Demands a Verdict,*:

> The apostles spent between 1.5 to 3 years with Jesus during His public ministry ...
>
> Although disillusioned at His untimely death, they became the first witnesses of the risen Jesus and they endured persecution; many subsequently experienced martyrdom, signing their testimony, so to speak, in their own blood ...
>
> Their willingness to die, indicates that they did not fabricate these claims; rather, without exception, they actually believed Jesus to have risen from the dead ... lending credibility to their claims about the veracity of the resurrection, which is fundamental to the case for Christianity.

Jesus foretold persecution in John 15:19-23:

> You are not of the world, but I chose you out of the world, therefore the world hates you ... If they persecuted Me, they will also persecute you ...
>
> But all these things they will do to you for My name's sake, because they

do not know Him who sent Me ... He who hates Me, hates My Father also.

Jesus said further in John 16:2-4:

The time cometh, that whosoever killeth you will think that he doeth God service. And these things will they do unto you, because they have not known the Father, nor me.

But these things have I told you, that when the time shall come, ye may remember that I told you of them.

Jesus forewarned in Matthew 24:9-14:

Then shall they deliver you up to be afflicted, and shall kill you: and ye shall be hated of all nations for my name's sake ...

And because iniquity shall abound, the love of many shall wax cold. But he that shall endure unto the end, the same shall be saved.

And this gospel of the kingdom shall be preached in all the world for a witness unto all nations; and then shall the end come.

Revelation 12:10-11 stated:

Now is come ... the kingdom of our God, and the power of his Christ: for the accuser of our brethren is cast down, which accused them before our God day and night. And they overcame him by the blood of the Lamb, and by the word of their testimony; and they loved not their lives unto the death.

In the first three centuries of the Church, there were ten major persecutions of Christians, in addition to innumerable minor ones:

1) Nero A.D. 54-68;

2) Domition A.D. 81- 96;

3) Trajan A.D. 98-117;

4) Antoninus Pius & Marcus Aurelius A.D. 138-180;

5) Severus A.D. 193 - 211;

6) Maximus A.D. 235-238;

7) Decius A.D. 249-251;

8) Valerian A.D. 253-260;

9) Aurelian A.D. 274-287;

10) Diocletian A.D. 292-304.

The government issued mandates making it a criminal act for Christians to assemble. Believers risked their lives every time they met. The Christian experience was an intensely personal relationship with the Lord and other believers, being prepared to die at any moment.

They gathered in small groups, often in catacombs – caves and tunnels carved under cities. Meetings were raided by police, believers were arrested, interrogated in secret hearings, thrown in jail, dragged before courts, ordered to deny their faith or die in shameful public spectacles like being fed to lions in the Colosseum.

# DIOCLETIAN

Emperor Diocletian lost battles in Persia. His generals blamed the defeat on the army's neglect of worshiping Roman gods. Diocletian ordered all military personnel and state employees to worship the Roman gods. This forced Christian soldiers to either go out of the military or into the closet.

In 286 A.D., Diocletian killed the entire Theban Legion of 6,000 Roman soldiers who had converted to Christianity because they would not worship the Roman gods.

After purging Christians from the military and government agencies, Diocletian surrounded himself with anti-Christian advisers. In 303 A.D., he consulted the Oracle Temple of Apollo at Didyma, which told him to initiate a great empire-wide persecution of Christians.

Diocletian revoked the tolerance issued by the previous Emperor Gallienus in 260 A.D., and then used the military to force the entire Roman Empire to return to worshiping pagan gods.

What followed was a decade of the worst and most intense persecution of Christians to that date.

Diocletian had his military go systematically, province by province, arresting church leaders, burning Scriptures, forbidding gatherings and destroying church buildings. He ordered the beautiful new church at Nicomedia torn down.

Christians were deprived of official ranks, lost jobs, imprisoned, had their tongues cut out, were boiled alive, and even decapitated.

From Europe to North Africa, thousands were martyred. The faithful cried out in prayer. Suddenly, Diocletian was struck with an intestinal disease so painful that he abdicated the throne, May 1, 305 A.D. The next emperor, Gelarius continued the persecution, but he too was struck with the intestinal disease and died in 311.

In 312 A.D, Emperor Constantine defeated Emperor Maxentius at the Battle of Rome's Milvian Bridge. Constantine issued the Edit of Milan in 313 A.D, ending the persecution.

Commenting on persecutions was Secretary of State William Jennings Bryan, the Democrat Party's Presidential candidate in 1896, 1900, and 1908. He stated in his speech, "The Prince of Peace," *New York Times*, September 7, 1913:

> I can imagine that the early Christians who were carried into the Colosseum to make a spectacle for those more savage than the beasts, were entreated by their doubting companions not to endanger their lives.
>
> But, kneeling in the center of the

arena, they prayed and sang until they were devoured ...

Bryan continued:

How helpless they seemed, and, measured by every human rule, how hopeless was their cause!

And yet within a few decades the power which they invoked proved mightier than the legions of the Emperor, and the faith in which they died was triumphant o'er all the land ...

They were greater conquerors in their death than they could have been had they purchased life.

It takes courage to walk in faith: Joshua 1:9 admonished:

Be strong and of a good courage; be not afraid, neither be thou dismayed: for the LORD thy God is with thee whithersoever thou goest.

Revelation 21:8 (NASB, KJV) lists cowards as the first ones thrown in the lake of fire:

But the cowardly [fearful], unbelieving, abominable, murderers, sexually immoral, sorcerers, idolaters, and all liars shall have their part in the lake which burns with fire and brimstone, which is the second death."

# WHAT KING BELIEVED, KINGDOM HAD TO BELIEVE

Throughout history, kings did not allow their subjects to believe something different than they did. In the 6th century B.C., Nebuchadnezzar of Babylon threw Shadrach, Meshach, and Abednego into the fiery furnace for not worshiping his statue, but the Lord delivered them.

In 527-565 A.D., Byzantine Roman Emperor Justinian the Great issued his famous *Codex Justinius* containing laws governing both church and state, based on the theology that Christ has both a divine nature and a human nature.

In Western Europe, there was a thousand-year tug-of-war between kings attempting to control the church by appointing bishops; and Popes attempting to control the state by witholding communion from kings and threatening excommunication.

When the Reformation happened in 1517, many kings viewed this as an opportunity to break from Rome and rule both their state and the church within it. This was codified in 1555 with the Peace of Augsburg, which contained the phrase, *cuius regio, euius religio*, meaning "whose is the reign, his is the religion."

What the king believed his kingdom had to

believe. Not to believe as your king was considered treason, punishable by death. Thousands were persecuted for conscience sake, displaced in mass migrations, or killed in wars.

❧

## JOHN WYCLIFFE

What is rare in history is people ruling themselves without a king and having freedom to believe as they chose. Where did the idea of self-government come from? To answer that, some history is necessary.

In the Middle Ages, pre-Reformation religious movements were led by:

• St. Francis of Assisi (1181-1226) and the Poor Franciscans;

• Peter Waldo (1140-1205) and the Waldensians of the Italian and French Alps;

• Friends of God in Basel, Strasbourg and Cologne, led by Miester Eckhart (1260-1328), Johannes Tauler (1300-1361), and Henry Suso (1295-1366).

In England, a pre-Reformation leader was John Wycliffe (1328-1384), a priest and scholar.

He entered the political discussion of his day by writing *De civili dominio* ("On Civil Dominion") in 1377, calling for the king to divest of church property, and examining the circumstances in which a leader may appropriately possess authority over lesser subjects.

In *Dominium,* Wycliffe treaded on politically dangerous grounds. He argued that an injury committed by a king against a subject should be patiently submitted to but an injury committed by a king against God should be resisted, even to death.

He taught that if kings or popes sin, they forfeit their divine right to be obeyed. This influenced the Lollards, Hussites and later Reformers.

Wycliffe aimed to replace the existing religious hierarchy with "poor priests" bound by no formal vows or consecration, who traveled as itinerant preachers among the common people, preaching in their own language "God's law, without which no one could be justified."

Pope Gregory XI issued a papal bull labeling Wycliffe's followers with the name "Lollards," an opprobrious epithet meaning "idle babbler."

Wycliffe wrote:

> Trust wholly in Christ; rely altogether on his sufferings; beware of seeking to be justified in any other way than by his righteousness. Faith in our Lord Jesus Christ is sufficient for salvation.

Wycliffe influenced a priest in Czech Bohemia,

Jan Hus (1370-1415), who began the Hussite movement.

Wycliffe's Bible translations were hand-copied as he lived before Johannes Gutenberg invented Europe's metal, movable-type printing press. His works were ordered to be collected and burned, resulting in few copies surviving. After the invention of the printing press, Reformation ideas quickly spread far and wide.

# LUTHER'S FAITH

In 1452, Muslim Turks conquered Constantinople, cutting off Europe's land routes east to India and China. This motivated Columbus to seek a westward sea route, sailing from Spain in 1492. Then, in 1497, Vasco de Gama left Portugal and sailed around South Africa to India.

Greek scholars fleeing the Turkish invasion of the Byzantine Empire arrived in Europe, carrying their Greek art, architecture, and literature, beginning the Renaissance. They also brought their Greek Old and New Testament Scriptures, laying the foundation for the Reformation.

A notable theologian was Dutch priest Desiderius Erasmus (1460-1526), who published the first Latin-Greek translation of the New

Testament in 1516, *Novum Instrumentum omne.*

He corresponded with Henry VIII's Catholic Chancellor, Sir Thomas More, and with an Augustinian monk in Germany, Martin Luther. Erasmus differed with Luther, preferring to reform the Church from within rather than leaving it.

After studying the Scriptures, Luther explained:

> I greatly longed to understand Paul's Epistle to the Romans and nothing stood in the way but that one expression, "the justice of God," because I took it to mean that justice whereby God is just and deals justly in punishing the unjust.
>
> My situation was that, although an impeccable monk, I stood before God as a sinner troubled in conscience, and I had no confidence that my merit would assuage him.
>
> Therefore I did not love a just and angry God, but rather hated and murmured against him. Yet I clung to the dear Paul and had a great yearning to know what he meant ...

He continued:

> Night and day I pondered until I saw the connection between the justice of God and the statement "The just shall live by faith." Then I grasped that the justice of God is that righteousness by which through sheer grace and mercy God

justifies us through faith.

Thereupon I felt myself to be reborn and to have gone through open doors into paradise. The whole of Scripture took a new meaning, and whereas before "the justice of God" had filled me with hate, now it became inexpressibly sweet in greater love. This passage of Paul became to me a gate to heaven ...

Luther concluded:

If you have a true faith that Christ is your Savior, then at once you have a gracious God, for faith leads you in and opens up God's heart and will, that you should see pure grace and over-flowing love.

This it is to behold God in faith that you should look upon his fatherly, friendly heart, in which there is no anger nor ungraciousness.

He who sees God as angry does not see him rightly but looks only on a curtain, as if a dark cloud had been drawn across his face.

# LUTHER'S 95 THESES

On October 31, 1517, Martin Luther tacked 95 debate questions, or "theses," on the door of All Saints Church in Wittenberg, Saxony-Anhalt,

Germany. This began the Reformation.

His initial objection was to the methods employed by Johann Tetzel to sell indulgences. Luther was then fiercely attacked by Johann Eck.

In 1521, the 34-year-old Martin Luther was summoned to stand trial before the most powerful king of that era, 21-year-old Holy Roman Emperor Charles V.

He ruled "the empire on which the sun never sets," spanning nearly 2 million square miles, including Spain, the Holy Roman Empire in Europe from Germany to northern Italy, Austrian lands, Burgundian Low Countries, and the southern Italian kingdoms of Naples, Sicily and Sardinia, as well as colonies in America and the Caribbean. The Philippines were named after his son, King Philip II.

At Luther's trial, called Diet of Worms, Charles dismissed Luther's points as "an argument between monks" and ordered him to recant without having had his theses addressed.

Luther reportedly declared:

> Unless I am convicted by Scripture and plain reason (I do not accept the authority of popes and councils because they have contradicted each other), my conscience is captive to the Word of God. I cannot and will not recant anything, for to go against conscience

*Silence Equals Consent*

is neither right nor safe. So help me God. Amen.

Luther's collected works recorded his closing line as, "Here I stand, I can do no other, so help me God. Amen."

A quote attributed to him regarding not being silent was published in the Weimar Ausgabe edition of Luther's works (*D. Martin Luther's Werke: kritische Gesamtausgabe,* publisher Hermann Böhlau Nachfolger, 1933, Briefwechsel, 18 volumes, 3. Band, ed., 81-82):

> It does not help that one of you would say: "I will gladly confess Christ and His Word on every detail, except that I may keep silent about one or two things which tyrants may not tolerate" ...
>
> For whoever denies Christ in one detail or word has denied the same Christ ... in all details, since there is only one Christ in all His words, taken together or individually.

Luther was declared outside the protection of law. He was kidnapped and hid by Frederick III of Saxony in Wartburg Castle, where he translated the New Testament into German. He wrote:

> The Bible was written for men with a head upon their shoulders.

Luther wrote of the importance of education:

> I am much afraid that schools will

prove to be the great gates of hell unless they diligently labor in explaining the Holy Scriptures, engraving them in the hearts of youth.

I advise no one to place his child where the scriptures do not reign paramount. Every institution in which men are not increasingly occupied with the Word of God must become corrupt.

As the Reformation spread, it unintentionally fueled an uprising called the German Peasants' War in 1524. Mobs of poor peasants threatened the aristocratic ruling class. The revolt was put down with over 100,000 peasants slaughtered.

Meanwhile, in 1527, Charles V's unruly troops sacked Rome "raping, killing, burning, stealing, the like had not been seen since the Vandals," and imprisoned Pope Clement VII for six months.

This was the same Pope who refused to annul the marriage of Charles V's aunt, Catherine of Aragon, and Henry VIII, resulting in Henry's breaking from Rome to start the Church of England.

Charles V presided over the Council of Trent (1545-1563) which began the Counter-Reformation to bring Protestant countries back under the Catholic Church. He oversaw the Spanish colonization of the Americas, yielding to the pleadings of the priest Bartolome' de Las Casas to outlaw enslavement of native Americans.

He used gold from the New World to fight the Turkish Ottoman expansion into Europe.

∽§

# SULTAN'S ISLAMIC INVASION

Catholic France and Catholic Spain were rival empires. At the Battle of Pavia, February 25, 1525, the King of France, Francis I, was captured and handed over to Charles V. From prison, he wrote to his mother, "all is lost, save honor."

After some concessions, giving up claims to various lands, Francis was released. He immediately caused a scandal in Europe by making an alliance with Spain's biggest enemy – Ottoman Sultan Suleiman the Magnificent.

Francis I also sent Verrazzano to explore the present-day New York City area in 1524, and in 1534, sent Jacques Cartier to explore Quebec.

Francis ordered the punishment of religious dissidents, such as the 1545 Massacre of Merindol against the pre-Reformation religious group Waldensians, founded by Peter Waldo in 1173.

Sultan Suleiman the Magnificent's fleets, now allied with France, dominated the Mediterranean Sea, the Red Sea and the Persian Gulf. He controlled the Middle East and North Africa.

Suleiman invaded Christian Hungary, Christian

Serbia, and the Christian Spanish–Habsburg Austria, laying siege to Vienna in 1529.

Martin Luther considered the Sultan's armies as judgments from God on Europe for its sins, in accordance with Deuteronomy 28. If a nation "shalt hearken diligently unto the voice of the Lord thy God ... all these blessings shall come on thee," but if a nation does not hearken to the voice of the Lord, "all these curses shall come upon thee," including:

> The stranger that is within thee shall get up above thee very high; and thou shalt come down very low ... and shall pursue thee, and overtake thee, till thou be destroyed.

How did God judge ancient Israel when it sinned? He let the strangers invade: Philistines, Edomites, Moabites, Ammonites. Egyptians, Assyrians, Babylonians, and others. When Israel repented, God raised up deliverers.

Luther wrote in *On War Against the Turk*, 1529:

> The Turk is the rod of the wrath of the Lord our God ... If the Turk's god, the devil, is not beaten first, there is reason to fear that the Turk will not be so easy to beat ... Christian weapons and power must do it ...

> [The fight against Turks] must begin with repentance, and we must reform our lives, or we shall fight in vain ...

> Every pastor and preacher ought diligently to exhort his people to repentance and to prayer.

> They ought to drive us to repentance by showing our great and numberless sins and our ingratitude, by which we have earned God's wrath and disfavor, so that he justly gives us into the hands of the devil and the Turk.

John Calvin wrote to Philip Melanchthon in 1543, (*Selected Works of John Calvin: Tracts & Letters*, I: 373):

> I hear of the sad condition of your Germany! ... The Turk again prepares to wage war with a larger force. Who will stand up to oppose his marching throughout the length and breadth of the land, at his mere will and pleasure?

# SULEIMAN'S INVASION HELPED THE REFORMATION

In an unanticipated way, Sultan Suleiman's invasion helped the Reformation. The Ottoman army was so formidable that it put Charles V in a double dilemma — trying to stop the Reformation on the inside of Europe while at the same time trying to stop the Ottoman invasion from the outside of Europe.

After decades of trying to stop both, he realized he needed help from the Lutheran kings. In an effort to unite the Holy Roman Empire against the Islamic invasion, Charles agreed to a truce recognizing Protestants.

Eric W. Gritisch wrote in *Martin-God's Court Jester: Luther in Retrospect* (PA: Fortress, 1983):

> Afraid of losing the much-needed support of the German princes for the struggle against the Turkish threat from the south, Emperor Charles V agreed to a truce between Protestant and Catholic territories in Nuremberg in 1532 ...
>
> Thus the Lutheran movement was, for the first time, officially tolerated and could enjoy a place in the political sun of the Holy Roman Empire.

When Lutheran German princes still hesitated, Charles V agreed to the Peace of Augsburg, September 25, 1555, with its Latin phrase, *cuius regio, eius religio*, meaning "whose is the reign his is the religion."

This allowed each king to decide what was to be believed in his kingdom. Some stayed Catholic and others became Lutheran, but whatever the king believed, his kingdom had to believe.

A month later, October 25, 1555, suffering from severe gout, Charles abdicated his throne and lived out his life secluded in the monastery of Yuste, leaving his son Philip II to rule.

❧

# HENRY VIII

In England, Henry VIII married Catherine of Aragon, the daughter of Ferdinand and Isabella of Spain, and the aunt of Charles V.

After 18 years, Catherine had a daughter, Mary, but no son. Wanting a male heir, Henry sought an annulment. When Pope Clement VII denied it, Henry broke from Rome and placed himself as the head of the Anglican Church.

He married his second wife, Anne Boleyn, who had a daughter Elizabeth I. Unfortunately, Henry soon had Anne beheaded. His next wife, Jane Seymour, had his only son, Edward VI.

The fate of Henry VIII's six wives were:

1) Catherine of Aragon, divorced;

2) Anne Boleyn, beheaded;

3) Jane Seymour, died;

4) Anne of Cleves, divorced;

5) Catherine Howard, beheaded;

6) Catherine Parr, survived.

In 1534, Henry demanded English subjects take the Oath of Supremacy:

> I (state your name) do utterly testify and declare in my Conscience, that the King's Highness is the only Supreme Governor of this Realm ... in all Spiritual or Ecclesiastical things ... So help me God.

When Henry's High Lord Chancellor, Sir Thomas More, a Catholic, refused to take the Oath, Henry had him executed. His last words were: "I die the King's good servant, and God's first."

Henry executed other Catholics, including John Fisher, Margaret Pole, and 18 Carthusian Martyrs. Cardinal Thomas Wolsey died before he could be executed.

Henry executed Protestants, including William Tyndale, Thomas Cromwell, Henry Howard, and lesser-known individuals such as George and Jane Boleyn, Anne Askew, and Elisabeth Barton.

# EDWARD VI, MARY I & ELIZABETH I

After Henry's death, his only son, Edward VI, became King of England.

At this turbulent time, a young man named John Knox (1514-1572) was arrested in Scotland and sentenced in 1547 as a galley slave on a French ship. Sailing from Scotland,

John Knox looked up as they passed St. Andrews and said:

> I see the steeple of that place where God first in public opened my mouth to glory; and I am fully persuaded ... I shall not depart this life till my tongue shall glorify his godly name in the same place.

After two years, John Knox was released and allowed to live in England. He rose to be the royal chaplain of young King Edward VI. Knox helped with writing the *Book of Common Prayer.*

When King Edward died, his half-sister, Queen Mary I, took the throne and attempted to bring England back under the Catholic Church.

She put her half-sister Elizabeth in the Tower of London in 1554. She executed Lady Jane Grey – the Nine Day Queen, and 300 others resulting in the disparaging epithet "Bloody Mary."

She ordered burned at the stake the Oxford Martyrs: Archbishop of the Anglican Church Thomas Cranmer; Anglican Bishop of London Nicholas Ridley; and Anglican Bishop Hugh Latimer, who had been Edward VI's chaplain.

Facing execution, October 16, 1555, Latimer exhorted Bishop Nicholas Ridley:

> Play the man, Master Ridley. We shall this day light such a candle, by God's grace, in England, as I trust shall never be put out.

John Knox escaped England with other Protestant scholars to Geneva, Switzerland. There they met Reformer John Calvin (1509–1564), and participated in creating the Geneva Bible.

Through Knox, Calvin's beliefs influenced Scotland, and in addition, the millions of Scots, Scots-Irish, Puritan and Presbyterian immigrants who came to America.

When Mary died in 1558, after reigning only five years, Elizabeth I became Queen of England.

When Spanish and Italian troops plotted to help Ireland break from Anglican English control in 1569, Elizabeth responded by attempting to subdue Ireland.

Elizabeth sent Sir Francis Drake to circumnavigate the globe, 1577-1580. She sent Sir Walter Raleigh to found a colony in America in 1584, which he named "Virginia" after virgin Queen Elizabeth. Elizabeth even attended some of Shakespeare's plays, notably *The Merry Wives of Windsor* and *Love's Labor's Lost*.

# IRON DUKE OF ALBA & THE SPANISH FURY

Suleiman the Magnificent was succeeded by

his son, Selim II. In 1571, Selim sent his navy to threaten Rome. Philip II, son of Charles V, helped in the defense. He had his 24-year-old half-brother, Don Juan of Austria, lead the Holy League navy.

Pope Pius V used his influence to get Catholic states to join Spain in a Holy League: Naples, Sicily, Venice, Genoa, Sardinia, Savoy, Urbino, Papal States, German and Croatian kingdoms.

On October 7, 1571, the largest, most decisive sea battle on the Mediterranean took place – the Battle of Lepanto off the western coast of Greece.

Don Juan and the Holy League's 212 ships with 68,000 soldiers defeated Ali Pasha and the Ottoman Turks' 251 ships with 82,000 soldiers.

Instead of capitalizing on the victory and freeing the Mediterranean from Islamist control, Philip II sent the Iron Duke of Alba in 1572 to carry out the Spanish Fury — a military campaign which killed ten thousand Dutch Reformed Protestants in Antwerp, Netherlands.

Spanish soldiers pillaged nonstop for three days the city of Mechelen. The rape and slaughter was so complete "that no nail was left in the wall."

The Dutch cities of Diest, Roermond, and Guelders were conquered. The entire population of the city of Zutphen was massacred. At Naarden, though inhabitants surrendered, they were all executed save for 60 people.

Haarlem agreed to surrender after a seven month siege and pay an enormous ransom, but Spanish soldiers still beheaded all the defenders or tied them back-to-back and threw them into the Spaarne River.

When Queen Elizabeth I sent help to the Dutch, Philip was incensed. He sent his Invincible Spanish Armada to sack England in 1588. The Spanish Armada was defeated with the help of the Dutch navy, and a timely hurricane.

A coin minted in Holland in 1588 had engraved on one side Spanish ships sinking and on the other side men kneeling under the inscription "Man Proposeth, God Disposeth."

∞

# ST. BARTHOLOMEW'S DAY MASSACRE

France's King Francis I died in 1547. He was succeeded by his son, Henry II, who married Catherine de' Medici, the daughter of Florentine banker Lorenzo de' Medici to whom Niccolo Machiavelli dedicated his book *The Prince.*

*The Prince,* 1513, exposed the tactics and intrigue for political power of Cesare Borgia, the illegitimate son of Pope Alexander VI, whose career went from being an 18-year-old cardinal to a mercenary military captain for Francis I's father.

Henry II suppressed Huguenots, who took their name from Besançon Hugues, the chief magistrate of Geneva, Switzerland, who was a follower of John Calvin.

After Henry II's death in 1559, his wife, Catherine de' Medici, ruled France through her teenage son, Francis II. At age 14, Francis was put in an arranged marriage with 15-year-old Mary, Queen of Scots. France and Scotland were allies against England since 1295.

At age 16, Francis II died and Mary was sent back to Scotland. Catherine de' Medici ruled France through her second son, 10-year-old Charles IX.

By this time, around ten percent of France had become Huguenot.

In 1572, Catherine de' Medici arranged a big wedding in Paris of her daughter Margaret to Henry of Navarre, the main Huguenot leader.

A few days after the wedding, on St. Bartholomew's Day, August 23, 1572, Catherine had her soldiers pull chains across the streets to prevent carriages from riding out of the city. Her soldiers went house-to-house, killing 30,000 Huguenot leaders. Their bodies were collected in carts and thrown into the Seine River. Henry of Navarre and his bride Margaret, barely escaped.

The killing of Huguenots spread in a War of Religion across France, killing 2 to 4 million.

∽

# MARY, QUEEN OF SCOTS & REFORMER JOHN KNOX

In 1561, having returned to Scotland, Mary, Queen of Scots, was preached to by the Presbyterian Reformer John Knox.

Knox had returned from Geneva to Scotland two years earlier in 1559 after the death of England's Catholic Queen Mary I and the coronation of Anglican Queen Elizabeth I.

In Scotland, Knox's preaching in St. Andrews stirred up anti-Catholic fervor. Catholic churches were vandalized and statues smashed.

In 1560, Knox was instrumental in having the Scottish Parliament officially accept the Presbyterian Church. Knox declared:

> A man with God is always in the majority.

Knox criticized the young Catholic Mary, Queen of Scots, who had just returned from France.

Mary's life was tragic. She married Lord Darnley in 1565, but he became jealous of Mary's private secretary, David Rizzio, and had

*Silence Equals Consent*

him murdered. Darnley was then suspiciously killed later in an explosion. The chief suspect in his murder was the Earl of Bothwell, who manipulated Mary into marrying him a month later.

This upheaval resulted in the Scottish Parliament forcing Mary to abdicate her throne. She was replaced by her and Lord Darnley's infant son, James. At the age of 13 months, James was crowned King James VI of Scotland, with John Knox giving the coronation sermon.

The Earl of Bothwell tried to raise forces to return Mary, Queen of Scots, to her throne, but he was captured in Norway and died in prison.

Mary, Queen of Scots, fled to England in 1568 to be protected by her cousin, Queen Elizabeth I.

Elizabeth felt threatened by Mary, as she had a claim to the English throne through her great-grandfather King Henry VII. Elizabeth ended up holding Mary in forced custody for 19 years.

In 1587, Elizabeth was made aware of a plot against her, which questionably implicated her captive Catholic cousin Mary, Queen of Scots. Tragically, Elizabeth signed the order for Mary to be executed. Catholics in England then went into hiding or fled. Large numbers of priests in England were captured and executed. This led to the Catholic King of Spain, Philip II, sending his invincible Spanish Armada in the failed attempt to conquer England in 1588.

Just as Spain's threat led to Francis I having France make a treaty with the Ottoman Empire in 1536, Spain's threat led to Queen Elizabeth making a treaty with Moroccan ruler Mulai Ahmad al-Mansur and Ottoman Sultan Murad III.

Murad thought Islam and Protestantism had "much more in common than either did with Roman Catholicism, as both rejected the worship of idols."

As Providence would have it, when Elizabeth died in 1603, the son of Mary-Queen of Scots, James I, was made King of England, Ireland, Wales and Scotland.

An observation of this era is that Catholics killed Protestants, and Protestants killed Catholics. French and Spanish Catholics killed each other. Anglican Protestants killed Presbyterian and Puritan Protestants, and vice versa. Turks and Christians killed each other. A lot of killing was going on, with blame to go around.

The purpose of reciting this history is not meant to reopen wounds of past religious conflicts but to trace how the founders of America broke away from powerful kings to set up a unique system where people ruled themselves without a king.

# COVENANT CHURCH

# JOHN CALVIN

With kings and queens killing subjects who believed differently than they did, in Geneva, Switzerland, was French pastor and theologian John Calvin, who wrestled with Romans 13:

> Let everyone be subject to the governing authorities, for there is no authority except that which God has established. The authorities that exist have been established by God.

For most of world history the "governing authorities" were monarchs, some good and some bad. Subjects were required to submit to their mandates. There is a problem, though, if the "governing authority" literally has a mandate to kill your wife and family? Are you supposed to submit to that?

Reformers who "protested" were labeled "Protestants." In addition to Calvin were Thomas Cranmer, John Knox, Philip Melanchthon, William Tyndale, Huldrych Zwingli, and others.

John Adams gave them credit in *A Dissertation on the Canon and Feudal Law*, 1765:

> Desire of dominion ... becomes an encroaching, grasping, restless, and ungovernable power ... Tyranny, cruelty,

and lust ... was soon adopted by almost all the princes of Europe ... The people were held in ignorance ... till God in his benign Providence raised up the champions who began and conducted the Reformation.

From the time of the Reformation to the first settlement of America, knowledge gradually spread in Europe, but especially in England; and in proportion as that increased and spread among the people ... tyranny ... lost ... strength.

Calvin wrote in *Institutes on the Christian Religion*, 1536:

The first duty of subjects towards their rulers is to entertain the most honorable views of their office, recognizing it as a delegated jurisdiction from God ...

We are always to make this exception ... that such obedience is never to lead us away from obedience to Him, to whose will the desire of all kings ought to be subject ...

We are subject to the men who rule over us, but subject only in the Lord. If they command anything against Him let us not pay the least regard to it.

This is the same line of reasoning as Ephesians 6:1, "Children obey your parents." But what if there is a bad parent who tells their child to sell themselves into prostitution and kill the neighbor. Is the child supposed to obey that parent? No!

The child is to obey the parent as long as the parent is telling them to do something that lines up with God's word. Likewise, one is to obey the government as long as the government is telling them to do something that lines up with God's word.

Think of it. Why would God tell you to do something in His word and then tell you to submit to a government that tells you not to do what He just got done telling you to do?

This is what Rev. Martin Luther King, Jr., wrote in his "Letter from Birmingham Jail," 1963:

> One may well ask: "How can you advocate breaking some laws and obeying others?" The answer lies in the fact that there are two types of laws: just and unjust …
>
> One has not only a legal but a moral responsibility to obey just laws. Conversely, one has a moral responsibility to disobey unjust laws. I would agree with St. Augustine that "an unjust law is no law at all."
>
> How does one determine whether a law is just or unjust? A just law is a man-made code that squares with the moral law or the law of God.

Calvin wrote in *Readings on Prophet Daniel* (Geneva, 1561), that when kings disobey God they "automatically abdicate their worldly power":

They are no longer worthy to be counted as princes ... When they raise themselves up against God ... it is necessary that they should in turn be laid low.

Calvin influenced the Puritans who developed a bottom-up form of government where citizens who read the Bible in their own language joined together in covenant with each other and with God to rule themselves without a king.

They taught that God had a perfect plan for your life, marriage, family, church, and also for government. Believers simply had to dig in the Scriptures, find God's plan and put it into place.

❧

## CALVINISTS

John Calvin's followers, called Calvinists, influenced the Puritans who sought to "purify" the Anglican Church from the inside.

In Scotland, Presbyterians were willing to acknowledge the king as their head, but they did not want his Anglican bishops overseeing them. They wanted their congregations independent.

Following Puritans and Presbyterians were Pilgrims or "separatists," as they separated themselves, meeting in secret small groups.

The Calvinist plan of believers ruling

themselves as a congregation without a king transitioned into citizens ruling themselves in a covenant civil government without a king. For it to work, though, every citizen had to participate.

Historian James F. Cooper described Calvinists in *Tenacious of Their Liberties: The Congregationalists in Colonial Massachusetts. Religion in America.* (Oxford Univ. Press, 1999):

> Adherence to fundamental or 'higher' laws, strict limitations upon all human authority, free consent, local self-government, and, especially, extensive lay participation."

U.S. Secretary of the Navy George Bancroft wrote in *History of the United States* (1834–74), the first comprehensive history of America:

> He who will not honor the memory and respect the influence of Calvin knows little of the origin of American liberty.

# CALVINISTS INSPIRED BY THE HEBREW REPUBLIC

Where did the Calvinists get their ideas? From the Bible. The question is, though, what part of the Bible?

As Scriptures were translated from Hebrew,

Greek, Syriac, and Latin, into the various European languages, Catholic and Protestant scholars were not only thrilled they could read the Bible in their own languages, but they were fascinated with a particular part of the Bible.

That first 400 years after Israel had its exodus out of Egypt and entered the Promised Land – "The Hebrew Republic," c.1,400 B.C. to 1,000 B.C.

During this initial period, ancient Israel had the most unique form of government — a covenant of the people with each other and with God. The Hebrew Republic is considered the first instance in recorded human history of a nation with millions of people being ruled without a king.

Kings rule through fear. For people to rule themselves without a king they need to have virtue. Montesquieu, the most quoted source by the writers of the U.S. Constitution after the Bible, wrote in *The Spirit of the Laws*, 1748:

> Of a despotic government, that a single person ... rule according to his own will and caprice ... He who commands the execution of the laws generally thinks himself above them, there is less need of virtue than in a popular government ...
>
> As virtue is necessary in a republic ... so fear is necessary in a despotic government ...

The Hebrew Republic worked as long as the people had virtue. Everyone was taught to read so they could read the Law, and they followed it because they were personally accountable to God.

This inspired America's "one nation under God," a phrase that is more than a nice acknowledgment. It is the awareness that each individual is personally accountable to God.

∽

# WHAT WAS
# THE HEBREW REPUBLIC?

Eric Nelson wrote in *The Hebrew Republic – Jewish Sources and the Transformation of European Political Thought*:

> During the 16th and 17th centuries, Christian scholars began to regard the Hebrew Bible as a political constitution designed by God for the children of Israel ... Rabbinic materials became authoritative guides to the institutions and practices of the perfect republic.

Joel P. Kramer of ExpeditionBible.com explained how in 1896, archaeologist Flinders Petrie discovered the Stele of Pharaoh Merneptah, successor of Pharaoh Ramses the Great, which contained the earliest inscription of the name

"Israel" outside the Bible, dated 1210 B.C.

The Merneptah Stele told of the Pharaoh conquering kingdoms, with each depicted by a carved hieroglyph of a king on his throne. The hieroglyph for Israel was the symbol for "people."

Harvard President Rev. Samuel Langdon gave an address "The Republic of the Israelites an Example to the American States," June 5, 1788:

> Israelites may be considered as a pattern to the world in all ages ... (of) government ... on republican principles ... (with) laws; without which it must have degenerated immediately into ... monarchy ...
>
> How unexampled was this quick progress of the Israelites, from abject slavery, ignorance, and almost total want of order, to a national establishment perfected in all its parts far beyond all other kingdoms and states!
>
> From a mere mob, to a well regulated nation, under a government and laws far superior to what any other nation could boast!"

The Hebrew Republic was a covenant of millions of Israelites ruling themselves under God with no king. Everyone had to agree to participate.

Picture a triangle – each citizen receives rights from God and is fair to their neighbor because they are accountable to God, who made everyone in His image and is not a respecter of persons.

Each citizen receives blessings from God and voluntarily shares them with their neighbor because they are doing it as unto God.

Puritans rediscovered the ancient Hebrew covenant. A century after the Puritans was the Age of Enlightenment, where philosophers morphed "covenant" into "social contract."

∽

## CHRISTIAN HEBRAISTS

The Hebrew Republic was studied by scholars called "Christian Hebraists." They led intellectual thought in Europe from the 16th century Renaissance and Reformation to the 17th century Age of Enlightenment. Leading Hebraists were:

Thomas Erastus (1524–1583);

Bonaventure Vulcanius (1535–1614);

Joseph Scaliger (1540–1609);

Johannes van den Driesche (1550–1616);

Isaac Casaubon (1559–1614);

Johannes Buxtorf (1564–1629);

Daniel Heinsius (1580–1655);

Hugo Grotius (1583–1645);

John Selden (1584–1654);

Thomas Hobbes (1588–1679);

James Harrington (1611–1677);

Petrus Cunaeus (1586–1638), who wrote *The Hebrew Republic* in 1617; and John Sadler (1615–1674), whose sister, Ann, married John Harvard, namesake of Harvard University. Harvard students learned Hebrew, just as Oxford and Cambridge students did. Yale University had on its coat of arms the Hebrew *Urim and Thummin*, translated in Latin as *Lux et Veritas* and into English as "Light and Truth."

Christian Hebraists studied the Jewish historian Josephus (37–100 A.D.); the Jerusalem Talmud (2nd century A.D.); the Babylonian Talmud (4th century A.D.); Jewish philosopher Maimonides (1135–1204); and Rabbinic literature.

Enoch Cobb Wines wrote in *Commentaries on the Laws of the Ancient Hebrews, with an Introductory Essay on Civil Society & Government* (NY: Geo. P. Putnam & Co., 1853):

> A fundamental principle of the Hebrew government was ... the education of the whole body of the people; especially, in the knowledge of the constitution, laws and history of their own country.
>
> An ignorant people cannot be a free people. Intelligence is essential to liberty. No nation is capable of self-government, which is not educated to understand and appreciate its

responsibilities ...

Maimonides, in his treatise on the study of the law, says: "Every Israelite, whether poor or rich, healthy or sick, old or young, is obliged to study the law ... " He asks, "How long ought a man to pursue the study of the law?" and replies, "Till death ..."

E.C. Wines continued:

Moses ... intended that all his people should share in the management of the public affairs. He meant each to be a depositary of political power ... as a solemn trust ...

On the subject of education, he appears chiefly anxious to have his people instructed in the knowledge of ... their duties as men and citizens.

He ... (did not) desire to see the mass of the people shut out from all political power ... nor ... to see the power of the masses increased, irrespective of their ability to discharge so important a trust beneficially to the community.

In his educational scheme, power and knowledge went hand in hand. The possession of the latter was regarded as essential to the right use of the former ...

In proportion as this idea enters into the constitution of a state, tyranny will hide its head, practical equality will

*Silence Equals Consent*

be established, party strife will abate its ferocity, error, rashness, and folly will disappear, and an enlightened, dignified, and venerable public opinion will bear sway ...

It is political ignorance alone, that can reconcile men to ... surrender of their rights; it is political knowledge alone, that can rear an effectual barrier against the encroachments of arbitrary power and lawless violence.

# SELF–GOVERNMENT

All governments are on a spectrum with total government on one side and no government on the other.

With total government, power is hierarchical, concentrated into one person, a king, who will always favor family and friends. They are "more" equal. If you are not family or friends, you are less equal. If you are their enemy you are dead. It is treason. Or you are a slave.

Kings rule through fear. Subjects do what they say or they can be killed. Lord Acton wrote:

> Power corrupts and absolute power corrupts absolutely.

The opposite end of the spectrum is no government, where power is separated into the hands of the people. At the Tower of Babel, God limited Nimrod's power by scattering it. Jesus limited Caesar's power, saying:

> Render therefore unto Caesar the things which are Caesar's; and unto God the things that are God's (Matthew 22:21).

An illustration is holding up one hand as a fist and the other hand with your fingers apart, then back to the fist. That is world history. For most of world history, power is in the fists of kings, pharaohs, caesars, kaisers, sultans, and tsars.

In rare instances, like the Hebrew Republic, power is separated into the hands of the people. If the people do not have virtue, though, it turns into anarchy and they cry for a king to restore order.

In ancient Israel's case, people had virtue because everyone was taught the law, they believed God wanted them to be fair, and they believed God was watching them and would hold them accountable in the future.

An illustration is to imagine everybody downloads a behavioral app on their iPhone.

Instead of a GPS app telling you where to turn, this behavioral app tells you how to act in real time. It monitors your blood pressure and if it is going up, with your voice volume rising, and it sees that someone is in close proximity, it runs an algorithm and predicts you are about to lose your temper. It sends you an alert: bzzz bzzz – "Do not lose your temper!"

It monitors your bank account and sees it is a little low, and with geo-positioning, it locates that you are in an expensive store with no one in the vicinity, and it runs an algorithm and predicts you are being tempted to steal. It sends you an alert – bzzz bzzz – "Do not steal."

Well, that is like what the Law was to the Israelites. The Levite priests were like computer geeks who helped you to download apps from Apple Store or Google Play, Levites helped you download the Law app, line upon line, precept upon precept.

There is a question, though, even if you download the Law app, what would motivate you to follow it? Israel had the key ingredient: there is a God Who is watching everyone, who wants you to be fair, and Who will hold you accountable in the future.

If you have an opportunity to act unfairly towards your neighbor and you remember that God is watching you and He wants you to be fair, and that He will hold you accountable in the future. You hesitate. This is called having a "conscience."

Under the Hebrew Republic, Israel was able to

keep order in society with no king. No one needed to lock their doors. Women could go anywhere without fear.

The Law specifically said there is to be no respect of persons in judgment. Everyone was to be treated exactly the same. This was the beginning of the concept of equality. Not only was everyone taught the Law and motivated to follow it, everyone helped enforce it. There were no police in ancient Israel.

God knew the Israelites would sin, so rather than them live the rest of their lives anticipating judgment, once a year the High Priest offered the Day of Atonement sacrifice, Yom Kippur, and everyone's sins were forgiven for the past year and they started the new year off with a clean slate, a foreshadowing of the sacrifice of Jesus, "the Lamb of God who taketh away the sins of the world" (John 1:29).

# HEBREW REPUBLIC ENDED

In the Hebrew Republic, the people were in covenant with each other and with God. Each person got blessings from God and voluntarily shared them with their neighbor because they were doing it as unto God.

In the New Testament, Jesus said: "Whatever you do unto the least of these my brethren you have done unto me." You get rights from God and you are fair to your neighbor because you are doing it as unto God, who is not a respecter of persons in judgment.

When people sin, though, lawlessness and chaos spread. People panic in fear and let go of the rubber band allowing power to snap back into the fist of a king.

The Hebrew Republic lasted 400 years, till the priests neglected teaching the Law and chaos ensued. Eli, the High Priest, allowed his own sons to sleep with women in the very tent where the Ark of the Covenant was. Another Levite was a priest in the house of someone named Micah who had a silver graven image.

Another Levite had a concubine, yet the Law said a Levite was to marry a woman of his own tribe and this Levite was with a woman he is not even married to. He was not following the Law. Traveling, they stopped for the night, and tragically, sodomites surrounded the house and raped the poor concubine to death.

Then you read the verse: "Every man did what was right in his own eyes." (Judges 21:25) Why? Because the Levites neglected teaching the people what was right in the Lord's eyes!

The people then went to Samuel the prophet

and essentially said, this self-government system is not working. We want to be like the other countries. We want a king.

When chaos ensued, the people sinned, asking for a king. Samuel cried and the Lord told him:

> They have not rejected you, but they
> have rejected Me, that I should not reign
> over them (I Samuel 8:7, NKJV).

Samuel complied with the people's wishes and anointed Saul as king. Saul concentrated power and ruled as a tyrant. He became jealous of David, causing the young man to flee.

❧

# KING SAUL RULED AS A TYRANT

David fled from Saul and stopped at the city of Nob. He asked the priests for some bread and the sword of Goliath that was kept there. Unaware that David had fallen out of favor with Saul, the priests helped him. Doeg the Edomite saw this.

In I Samuel 22 (NIV), Saul was pouting that his son Jonathan was friends with David.

> No one tells me when my son makes
> a covenant with the son of Jesse. None
> of you is concerned about me or tells
> me that my son has incited my servant
> to lie in wait for me, as he does today."

But Doeg the Edomite, who was standing with Saul's officials, said,

"I saw the son of Jesse come to Ahimelek son of Ahitub at Nob. Ahimelek inquired of the Lord for him; he also gave him provisions and the sword of Goliath the Philistine."

Then the king sent for the priest Ahimelek son of Ahitub and all the men of his family, who were the priests at Nob, and they all came to the king. Saul said, "Listen now, son of Ahitub."

"Yes, my lord," he answered.

Saul said to him, "Why have you conspired against me, you and the son of Jesse, giving him bread and a sword and inquiring of God for him, so that he has rebelled against me and lies in wait for me, as he does today?"

Ahimelek answered the king,

"Who of all your servants is as loyal as David, the king's son-in-law, captain of your bodyguard and highly respected in your household? Was that day the first time I inquired of God for him? Of course not! Let not the king accuse your servant or any of his father's family, for your servant knows nothing at all about this whole affair."

But the king said,

"You will surely die, Ahimelek, you

and your whole family."

Then the king ordered the guards at his side:

"Turn and kill the priests of the Lord, because they too have sided with David. They knew he was fleeing, yet they did not tell me."

But the king's officials were unwilling to raise a hand to strike the priests of the Lord.

The king then ordered Doeg,

"You turn and strike down the priests."

So Doeg the Edomite turned and struck them down. That day he killed eighty-five men who wore the linen ephod. He also put to the sword Nob, the town of the priests, with its men and women, its children and infants, and its cattle, donkeys and sheep.

What just happened?

The soldiers were still operating under the old system, where each citizen was accountable to God to keep the Law, and the Law required two or more witnesses before someone could be condemned to death (Deuteronomy 17:6).

> At the mouth of two witnesses, or three witnesses, shall he that is worthy of death be put to death; but at the mouth of one witness he shall not be

put to death.

The soldiers hesitated because there was only one witness – Doeg. They still had a conscience.

The Law also instructed that a trial should be before "the elders of the city." Saul held no trial, but just commanded the priests be executed.

It is ironic that the priests who neglected teaching people the law were responsible for the chaos that led the people to ask for a king who turned around and killed the priests.

Pastors who teach believers not to be involved may be responsible for the chaos that results in people surrendering freedoms to a government which will persecute pastors. Uninvolved pastors may be creating the ungodly government which will persecute them.

Saul effectively told his soldiers to stop fearing God and instead fear him — stop having a conscience, just be a robot and obey mandates.

What Doeg the Edomite did was surrender his conscience to the government. If the government says kill priests, then kill priests.

Many citizens today are acting like Doeg. If the government says kill the baby in the womb, they kill it. If the government says there is no more male and female and use confusing pronouns, they comply. They are mush, like the Babylonians, who when Nebuchadnezzar blew his trumpets, they bowed.

Tyrannical governments always want to pressure citizens to surrender their common sense and deeply held religious convictions. *The Hill* reported October 6, 2023: "Hillary Clinton: MAGA 'cult members' need 'deprogramming':

> Former Secretary of State Hillary Clinton railed against supporters of former President Trump during a new CNN interview, comparing those who still support the former president after the Jan. 6, 2021, insurrection to members of a cult.
>
> "Maybe there needs to be a formal deprogramming of the cult members," she said in a clip released late Thursday.

Rather than *protecting* beliefs, tyrants want to *dictate* beliefs. Tyrants want "yes men" who fear them instead of God. Josephus wrote in *Antiquities of the Jews* (c. 94 A.D.):

> Nimrod ... gradually changed the government into tyranny, seeing no other way of turning men from the fear of God, but to bring them into a constant dependence on his power.

Where there is a king, only his will matters, especially since he commands the police and army.

In a sense, King Saul was the divider between England and America.

The kings of England looked to the Bible for their authority, but they looked to the King Saul period, and beyond, as the source of the divine right of kings.

Puritans looked to the Bible for their authority but they looked to the pre-King Saul period — the original 400 years in the Promised Land where people ruled themselves without a king – God's original plan.

Both of them claimed the Bible as their authority, but King James looked to post-King Saul and Puritans looked to pre-King Saul.

# WILLIAM TYNDALE'S BIBLE

An important factor to consider in self-government was the ability of the people to read the Bible, and which Bible translation.

A key translator of the Bible was William Tyndale. His Bible, published from 1522–1533, is considered the first translation in the English language which drew directly from Hebrew and Greek texts in addition to the Latin Vulgate. It was printed in mass quantities and smuggled from Europe back into England.

The word "church" does not appear in Tyndale's Bible. Instead he translated the Greek word *ekklesia* as "congregation" or "assembly." Though religious hierarchy of the day considered this radical and anti-clerical, reformers favored it.

Tyndale translated the Greek word *presbúteros* as "presbyter" or "elder" rather than "priest." He translated the Greek word *metanoeîte* as "repent" rather than "do penance." He used the word "love" rather than "charity."

In an era where only the clergy could read the Bible, Tyndale stated his goal was to "cause a boy that driveth the plough to know more scripture than the clergy of the day."

Tyndale personally translated the New Testament and was only able to translate portions of the Old Testament before he was betrayed, captured and martyred. Myles Coverdale completed Tyndale's translating work and published the Coverdale Bible.

A few years after Tyndale's death, Henry VIII wanted to break from Rome so he could divorce his wife Catherine of Aragon and marry Anne Boleyn. His advisors convinced him that a Bible in English would facilitate his break, so Henry authorized the Great Bible of 1539.

## GENEVA BIBLE

When Mary I, daughter of Henry VIII, became Queen of England, she wanted to bring the country back under the Roman Catholic Church. This led to Protestant Bible scholars, known as the Marian exiles, fleeing to Geneva, Switzerland.

There they met John Calvin and Theodore Beza, who had produced a French Bible in 1551.

In Geneva, English Bible scholars, which included William Whittingham, Miles Coverdale, Christopher Goodman, Anthony Gilby, Thomas Sampson and John Knox, translated the Geneva Bible, published in 1560.

It was smuggled back into England. After Mary I died, and Elizabeth I became Queen, the Bible scholars returned to England.

Since John Knox, who was from Scotland, was involved in creating the Geneva Bible, it was widely accepted in Scotland. In 1579, a law was passed requiring every home to purchase one.

The Geneva Bible was used by Shakespeare, Oliver Cromwell, John Knox, John Donne, John Bunyan, and carried by the Pilgrims on the *Mayflower* to America.

The Geneva Bible, in Ephesians 6:12, referred to wrestling against "worldly governors," calling them "the princes of the darkness of this world":

> For we wrestle not against flesh and blood, but against principalities, against powers, and against the worldly governors, the princes of the darkness of

this world, against spiritual wickedness, which are in the high places..

The Geneva Bible had explanatory notes in the margin which expressed Calvinistic views of the Church being believers in a covenant, and that is the state, monarchs should be obeyed only if they are submitted to God's Word.

*TIME* magazine published the article "Looking to Its Roots" (May 25, 1987):

> Ours is the only country deliberately founded on a good idea. That good idea combines a commitment to man's inalienable rights with the Calvinist belief in an ultimate moral right and sinful man's obligation to do good.
>
> These articles of faith, embodied in the Declaration of Independence and in the Constitution, literally govern our lives today.

# KING JAMES BIBLE

When Elizabeth died in 1603, James I, the son of Mary, Queen of Scots, was made King of England, Ireland, Wales and Scotland.

James had been raised by Scottish Presbyterian tutors who advocated limited government, but James rejected these concepts and wholeheartedly embraced "the divine right of kings."

James did not like the Geneva Bible as it was filled with margin notes which emphasized a congregation church structure and a limitation of the king's power.

He sought to replace it with a Bible with no margin notes, and have it be such a good translation that another would not be attempted.

He gave instructions to the translators:

> No marginal notes at all to be affixed, but only for the explanation of the Hebrew or Greek words, which cannot, without some circumlocution, so briefly and fitly be expressed in the text.

James also required of the translators, that:

> The old ecclesiastical words to be kept; as the word church, not to be translated congregation.

To his credit, he was responsible for arranging Anglican, Puritan and Presbyterian scholars to work together to produce the King James Bible – the best-selling and the most distributed book of all time.

James I is the namesake of Jamestown, Virginia – the first permanent English settlement in America.

In an effort to make Ireland more Protestant, James relocated some 200,000 Presbyterians from Scotland to Ulster, Ireland.

In the following years, crop failures, collapsing

linen trade, and increased rents caused nearly a million Scots and Scots–Irish Protestant Presbyterians to leave Ireland and immigrate to the American colonies, spreading the influence of John Calvin and John Knox in America.

∽

# FRANCE: AN ABSOLUTE MONARCHY

In France, Catherine de' Medici's second son Charles IX became king in 1560 at the death of his brother, Henry III. Under Catherine's direction, in 1562, Charles IX carried out massacres of Calvinist Huguenots at Vassy, Sens, Castelnaudary and Bar-sur-Seine. This was followed by massacres of tens of thousands of Huguenots all across France.

Henry III's mental and physical constitution began to fail, leading up to his death in 1574.

While dying, he cried to his nurse that the screams of the murdered Huguenots kept ringing in his ears: "What blood shed! What murders!" and "What evil counsel I have followed! O my God, forgive me ... I am lost! I am lost!" He yelled at his mother, "Who but you is the cause of all of this? God's blood, you are the cause of it all!" Catherine's cold response, as relayed by historian

Will Durant, was that she had a lunatic for a son.

Catherine's third son Henry III was king until his assassination by a Catholic zealot friar in 1589. That same year Catherine died.

The next king was Henry of Navarre, known as Good King Henry IV, who escaped the St. Bartholomew's Day Massacre. He tried to reconcile Catholics with Protestants by issuing the Edit of Nantes in 1598, which included:

> Freedom of conscience and the right to practice their religion (Protestantism) in certain specified towns and cities throughout France.

> The right to hold public office, including the right to serve as judges and administrators, without having to renounce their religion.

> The right to maintain their own schools and universities, and to receive government funding for them.

> The right to fortify their towns and cities for their own protection.

> The right to maintain their own military forces (known as "Huguenot militia"), which were to be paid for by the French government.

> The right to engage in certain specified trades and professions, including the manufacture and sale of textiles and arms.

The right to travel freely throughout France, without being subject to searches or seizures of their property.

The right to bury their dead in their own cemeteries.

Unfortunately, Good King Henry IV was assassinated in 1610 by a Catholic zealot. Henry's wife, Marie de' Medici ran France until her son, Louis XIII, turned 16. She recommended to him that Cardinal Richelieu serve as royal minister.

Richelieu, called l'*Éminence rouge*, established a royal monopoly by force. He concentrated so much power in the state that France became the definition of an "absolute monarchy."

Richelieu resisted Catholic Habsburg Spain, and in 1627, personally led the French army in laying siege to the Huguenot city of La Rochelle.

Richelieu's political intrigue was such that the King's mother, Marie de' Medici, tried to have him dismissed, but instead, he succeeded in having her banished in exile.

King Louis XIII sent Samuel de Champlain to settle New France – Canada. Louis XIII died in 1643.

His son, Louis XIV, took the throne and reigned nearly 73 years, considered the longest reign of any sovereign. It was *Le Grand Siècle*"– the Great Century. In 1682, he relocated the Royal Court to his enormous Palace of Versailles.

*Silence Equals Consent*

Louis XIV was called "The Sun King," as his subjects revolved around him like planets everyday. With complete centralized power, he was the ultimate "absolute monarch." When an administrator told him he could not do something because it was illegal, he replied, "It is legal because I wish it."

Louis XIV insisted on a perfect autocracy, recorded by Pierre-Édouard Lémontey as saying: "*L'État, c'est moi*" — "I am the state." He instituted a policy of government coercion called "dragonnades" to forcibly convert Protestants back to Catholicism.

In 1685, he ended all Protestant rights with his Edict of Fontainebleau, officially revoking the toleration of the Edict of Nantes.

# JAMES I, CHARLES I, & RELIGIOUS UNIFORMITY

Back in England, James I of England aspired to be an absolute monarch. He did not like Calvinist covenant congregation church structure but insisted upon the hierarchical church structure, with him at the top, ruling through mandates. He claimed the King was "master over every person."

In 1605, an assassination attempt was made

on James I in the Gun Powder Plot, led by Guy Fawkes, a supporter of Catholic Spain.

Fawkes and other conspirators smuggled 36 barrels of gunpowder into the cellar beneath Parliament's House of Lords, intending to blow it up on the day James was to give an address.

The plot was thwarted, but afterwards James I was so paranoid that he persecuted all dissenting religious groups, whether Catholic, Puritan, Presbyterian, or Separatist Pilgrim.

James I enforced The Act Against Puritans, 1593, punishing anyone who did not attend Church of England services for forty days, or who attended private services:

> (They) shall be committed to prison, there to remain without bail ... until they shall confirm and yield themselves to same church.

James demanded absolute religious uniformity. A person was not even allowed to make up their own prayers because they could make up one that is wrong, so the government wrote all the possible prayers down in *The Book of Common Prayer*.

When a person felt like praying, they were to just open it to the right page and read the prayer. Over 300 ministers who refused to use *The Book of Common Prayer* were suspended.

One of those suspended was John Robinson. In 1606, he joined John Smyth's Baptist Church till he formed his own, meeting at the home of William Brewster in Scrooby, England. A young man who joined the church was 16-year-old William Bradford.

In 1608, John Robinson and his Baptist separatist church fled to Holland. They came to be known as the Pilgrims. After 12 years, 102 of his church members sailed to America in 1620 aboard the *Mayflower*. They were "knit together as a body in ... covenant of the Lord ... tied to ... care of each other's good."

When King James died in 1625, his son, Charles I, took the throne. He increased demands for religious uniformity. Resistance grew.

In 1637, at the first public reading of *The Book of Common Prayer* in St. Giles Cathedral, in Edinburgh, Scotland, a market-woman named Jenny Geddes is said to have thrown her three-legged stool at the minister in protest.

This sparked into a riot that led to the Bishops' War of 1639, requiring all ministers to be ordained by the Bishop and use *The Book of Common Prayer*.

Then followed the Wars of the Three Kingdoms, 1639–1653. Anglicans fought three groups: England's Puritans, Scotland's Presbyterians, and Ireland's Catholics.

This conflict transitioned into several fronts: Catholics fought Charles I in the Irish Confederate

Wars, 1641–1653; and Puritans and Presbyterians joined in fighting Charles I in the First English Civil War, 1642–1646.

On the side of King Charles I were the Royalist Anglican "Cavaliers," and on the other side were Puritan Parliamentarians and Scottish Covenanters, led by Lord Fairfax and Oliver Cromwell.

When Charles I was about to be captured, he surrendered to Scotland and gave them a promise that if they would back him, he would respect their Presbyterian church structure with no bishops. Based on this promise, the Scots suddenly switched sides to fight to return King Charles to the throne.

Cromwell defeated the Scots and captured Charles I. Shortly after, Charles was beheaded in 1649.

The Scots then crowned Charles I's 21-year-old son, Charles II, as king in return for his promise to respect Presbyterian Church independence with no bishops. He later reneged on the promise.

Charles II was defeated in the Anglo–Scottish War and he fled to France in 1651 to be under the protection of his 13-year-old cousin, the absolute monarch, King Louis XIV.

# OLIVER CROMWELL & THE ENGLISH COMMONWEALTH

Oliver Cromwell led the Commonwealth of England from 1649 till his death in 1658. The Commonwealth was based on the Puritan covenant, a voluntary relationship with representatives, elected by the people, with God.

Puritan minister William Perkins stated in a sermon, 1624:

> We are by nature covenant creatures, bound together by covenants innumerable and together bound by covenant to our God ... Blest be the ties that bind us.

Cromwell refused to be king but instead took the title "Lord Protector." He let Jews back into England for the first time since King Edward I had expelled them in 1290.

During the Commonwealth of England, also called the "Interregnum," Oliver Cromwell demoted Anglican ministers, including Reverend Lawrence Washington, the great-great-grandfather of George Washington. This led to Lawrence's son, John Washington, becoming a merchant and sailing to Virginia in 1657.

When Puritan leader Oliver Cromwell died in 1658, his son Richard Cromwell could not hold the Commonwealth together.

The Commonwealth of England had been, in a sense, a temporary "American Experiment." It was a covenant form of self-government.

A royalist movement grew and in 1660, Charles II was brought back from exile in France and put on the throne, restoring England's monarchy.

# RETURN OF MONARCHY

Admiral William Penn, father of the Pennsylvania's founder, was key in bringing Charles II back from France. In return, the King knighted him "Sir" Admiral William Penn.

Os Guinness stated in an interview, "Thinking in Public," June 5, 2017:

> The covenantal ideas in England were the lost cause, sadly. They failed. The king came back.

Once the monarchy was reestablished, Charles II began royal retribution, arresting and killing those who took part in killing his father.

The purge broadened into a wave of persecution against non-Anglican, non-conformist Christians. These included: Catholics, Puritans, Separatists, Baptists, Scottish Covenanters, and other dissenters, who were spied upon, tracked, censored and arrested.

In 1662, Parliament passed the Act of Uniformity, which required all preachers to submit and believe exactly what the government told them to believe. If not, they would not be ordained by an Anglican bishop, a necessary requirement to be permitted to preach.

In 1665, Parliament passed the Five Mile Act, making it illegal for a dissenting preacher to preach within five miles of any town. If they did, they were arrested.

Small-group Bible studies and prayer meetings were called "conventicles," which comes from the word "covenant." Jesus said, "where two or three are gathered in my name, I am there in the midst."

In 1664, Parliament passed the Act of Conventicles, which made it illegal for five or more people to have a religious meeting apart from the Church of England.

If someone was caught with a small group making up prayers, the police, similar to the FBI, would bust into their house and arrest them, with the bishop assisting. They were brought to a secret government hearing room called the "Star Chamber" because it had stars on the ceiling.

Then, similar to January 6th-type hearings, they were threatened with long prison sentences unless they confessed to things they did not do.

Some were branded on the face as heretics or had their ears cut off. Then they were put in horrible jail cells for months or years. Prisoners were not even fed. They had to have some friend who missed them bring food or they would starve.

The Conventicle Act was changed to the Riot Act because you could be planning an insurrection in your little Bible study. The police would kick in the door, pull out a piece of paper and read the Riot Act, which said everyone must immediately disperse or they will be arrested, dragged to the Star Chamber, and thrown in prison. It was so severe that it became a feared expression — "Read them the Riot Act!"

King Charles II and King James II maintained a hierarchical, clergy–laity church structure. They imprisoned Quakers, crushed Catholic revolts in Ireland and tracked down and killed some 18,000 Scottish Presbyterians during "The Killing Time," 1680–1688.

Persecution continued into the next century, where in England's colony of Virginia, the town of Culpeper had the Anglican government arrest Baptist pastors.

Prior to the Revolution, James Madison wrote to William Bradford, January 24, 1774:

> There are at this time in the adjacent Culpeper County not less than 5 or 6 well meaning men in jail for publishing their religious sentiments which in the main are very orthodox.

# PRISONER FOR CONSCIENCE SAKE, JOHN BUNYAN

In 1644, at the age of 16, Bunyan joined the Puritan Parliamentary Army and fought under Oliver Cromwell during the First English Civil War. As a soldier, he escaped death several times. He wrote in *Grace Abounding*:

> When I was a Soldier, I, with others, were drawn out to go to such a place to besiege it; But when I was just ready to go, one of the company desired to go in my room, to which, when I had consented, he took my place; and coming to the siege, as he stood Sentinel, he was shot into the head with a Musket bullet and died.

After three years in the military, he returned to live in his cottage in the village of Elstow. Being poor and unskilled, he learned from his father the trade of a tinker.

His life changed when he married his young, pious wife. She had two books inherited from her father: Arthur Dent's *Plain Man's Pathway to Heaven*; and Lewis Bayly's *Practice of Piety*. Apart from that, the newly-weds owned little, "not having so much household–stuff as a dish or a spoon betwixt us both."

Their first daughter was blind, then they had

another daughter and two sons. They attended the non-conformist Bedford Free Church.

In 1657, at age 29, Bunyan became a Baptist minister. He was preaching in a farm house near Bedford, England, when it was raided by the police. He was arrested and dragged away, all because he was having an unauthorized religious meeting and for preaching without the permission of the government.

Bunyan wrote in *A Relation of My Imprisonment*:

> Upon the 12th of ... November 1660 ... the justice ... issued out his warrant to take me ... as if we that were to meet together ... to do some fearful business, to the destruction of the country ... when alas! the constable, when he came in, found us only with our Bibles in our hands, ready to speak and hear the word of God ...

> So I was taken and forced to depart ... But before I went away, I spake some few words of counsel and encouragement to the people, declaring to them ... that they would not be discouraged, for it was a mercy to suffer upon so good account ... We suffer as Christians ... better be the persecuted, than the persecutors.

Unfortunately, a resurgence of these tactics has been seen recently. As reported by *WND.com*, November 22, 2021; "So It Begins: FBI Raids

Home of Mom Who Protested School Board."

> On November 16, 2021, the FBI's heavily armed SWAT team broke down the door of a homeschool mom's house in suburban Colorado and handcuffed her while she was homeschooling her three children. They man-handled her 18-year-old daughter, dragging her up the stairs by her hoodie.
>
> The Administration's Attorney General targeted the mother because she had expressed her views regarding the curriculum used in public schools.

John Bunyan was imprisoned for twelve years, from 1660–1672, and again 1675–1676. During his imprisonment, he supported his family by making shoelaces. It was during this time that he wrote *The Pilgrim's Progress*, published in 1678.

*The Pilgrim's Progress* is an allegory of a pilgrim named Christian, who flees the City of Destruction and is directed by Evangelist to the straight and narrow path. He overcomes temptation, deception, depression, and persecution on his way to the Celestial City of Zion.

It has been translated into over 200 languages and, after the Bible, was the world's best-seller for hundreds of years. It has never been out of print. It was found in nearly every colonial New England home, along with the Bible and *Fox's Book of Martyrs*, 1563.

Bunyan described Christian crossing the doubts of the Slough of Despond and almost being led astray by Mr. Worldly Wiseman. He struggled to obey the legalistic rules of Mr. Legality till he was almost crushed by Mount Sinai. He was then directed by Evangelist to the King's Highway of Grace. He dodged the arrows shot by Beelzebub, till he "came at a place somewhat ascending, and upon that place stood a cross":

> So I saw in my dream, that just as Christian came up with the cross, his burden loosed from off his shoulders, and fell from off his back.

He almost turned back:

> Then said Christian, You make me afraid, but whither shall I fly to be safe? ... To go back is nothing but death; to go forward is fear of death, and life-everlasting beyond it. I will yet go forward ...

> Frighted with the sight of the lions ... Christian said to himself again, These beasts range in the night for their prey; and if they should meet with me in the dark ... how should I escape being by them torn in pieces? ...

> He lift up his eyes, and behold there was a very stately palace before him ... He entered into a very narrow passage ... he espied two lions in the way ... The porter at the lodge ... perceiving that

Christian made a halt as if he would go back, cried unto him, saying,

"Is thy strength so small? Fear not the lions, for they are chained, and are placed there for trial of faith where it is, and for discovery of those that had none. Keep in the midst of the path, and no hurt shall come unto thee."

At the Palace Beautiful, Christian was clothed in the Armor of God, and went on alone:

But now, in this Valley of Humiliation, poor Christian was hard put to it ... a foul fiend coming over the field to meet him; his name is Apollyon ... Then did Christian begin to be afraid, and to cast in his mind whether to go back or to stand his ground.

But he considered again that he had no armor for his back ... Therefore he resolved to venture and stand his ground ... The monster was hideous to behold; he was clothed with scales ... wings like a dragon, feet like a bear, and out of his belly came fire and smoke ...

Apollyon straddled quite over the whole breadth of the way, and said ... prepare thyself to die; for I swear by my infernal den, that thou shalt go no further; here will I spill thy soul ... And with that he threw a flaming dart at his breast; but Christian had a shield in his hand, with which he caught it ...

Apollyon as fast made at him, throwing darts as thick as hail; by the which, notwithstanding all that Christian could do to avoid it, Apollyon wounded him in his head, his hand, and foot ...

This sore combat lasted for above half a day, even till Christian was almost quite spent; for you must know that Christian, by reason of his wounds, must needs grow weaker and weaker ... Christian's sword flew out of his hand.

Then said Apollyon, "I am sure of thee now." And with that he had almost pressed him to death, so that Christian began to despair of life; but as God would have it, while Apollyon was fetching of his last blow, thereby to make a full end of this good man, Christian nimbly stretched out his hand for his sword, and caught it, saying ...

"Rejoice not against me, O mine enemy; when I fall I shall arise"; and with that gave him a deadly thrust, which made him give back ... And with that Apollyon spread forth his dragon's wings, and sped him away, that Christian for a season saw him no more.

Soon after, Christian met a fellow–pilgrim named Faithful, and the two traveled to Vanity Fair. They were enticed with every worldly temptation but stayed holy. The angered mob locked them in a cage and a rigged jury sentenced

Faithful to be martyred, yet Christian escaped.

He met another traveler, Hopeful. They hiked the straight and narrow path, but where it got rocky they saw a soft parallel path along the Hill Lucre. Taking it, they became trapped by Giant Despair and were chained in the dungeon of Doubting Castle.

The Giant put poison and a dagger in their cell and told them to commit suicide. Depressed, they sang, as the Apostle Paul did, "till almost the break of day":

> Christian ... half amazed, brake out in this passionate speech: – What a fool, quoth he, am I, thus to lie in a stinking dungeon, when I may as well walk at liberty! I have a key in my bosom, called Promise, that will, I am persuaded, open any lock in Doubting Castle."

They escaped, but were then almost led astray by Flatterer. Resisting sleep as they crossed the Enchanted Land, in the distance they saw Immanuel's Land.

Atheist met them, going in the opposite direction. He told them there was no Heaven and to turn back. Thankfully, they had been warned by Shepherds and continued on. Finally they came to the last test, the River of Death.

A man named Ignorance tried to get them into a ferry named Vain Hope, trusting in good works rather than God's grace. Christian and Hopeful instead began wading across. As it got deeper and deeper, they trusted in God's promises. Sinking under billowing waves, they were suddenly pulled out on the other side and ushered by angels into the Celestial City of Zion:

> Now ... behold a company of the heavenly host came out to meet them ... "These are the men that have loved our Lord when they were in the world, and that have left all for his holy name ... that they may go in and look their Redeemer in the face with joy ... Blessed are they which are called unto the marriage supper of the Lamb."

Franklin D. Roosevelt wrote January 19, 1936:

> When Theodore Roosevelt died, the Secretary of his class at Harvard, in sending classmates a notice of his passing, added this quotation from *Pilgrim's Progress*:

> "My sword I give to him that shall succeed me in my pilgrimage, and my courage and skill to him that can get it. My marks and scars I carry with me, to be a witness for me that I have fought His battles who now will be my rewarder.'"

*Silence Equals Consent*

❧

# *CHURCH INFLUENCED STATE*

# CHURCH STRUCTURE BECAME CIVIL STRUCTURE

French political writer, Montesquieu wrote of Europe in *The Spirit of the Laws*, 1748:

> When the Christian religion, two centuries ago, became unhappily divided into Catholic and Protestant, the people of the north embraced the Protestant, and those of the south adhered still to the Catholic.

> The reason is plain: the people of the north have, and will forever have, a spirit of liberty and independence, which the people of the south have not; and therefore a religion which has no visible head is more agreeable to the independence of the climate than that which has one ...

> When a religion is introduced and fixed in a state, it is commonly such as is most suitable to the plan of government there established.

After the Reformation, not only did denominations develop doctrine, they also developed different types of church government, each with their own advantages and disadvantages.

The purpose of this analysis is not to debate which form of church government is better, but rather to understand how the various church governments influenced the development of civil government in the American colonies.

Different structures may reach different people with the truth of Christ as Savior. Ephesians 4:15 (NIV) states:

Speaking the truth in love, we will grow to become in every respect the mature body of him who is the head, that is, Christ.

The Lord is able to use any structure where people strive to follow God's Word and the Holy Spirit. Conversely, the devil will try to infiltrate any church structure where people do not strive to follow God's Word and the Holy Spirit.

The four main categories discussed are: hierarchical; presbyter elders; congregational; and Quakers – a society of friends.

A hierarchical structure is where a person's relationship with God is through an episcopal organization, tracing itself through bishops in an apostolic succession back to the first century church. "Episcopal" means "relating to bishops."

The Anglican Church had this structure. In 1534, England had subjects take the Oath of Supremacy, accept the king as the head of both the state and the church. Under him was the Archbishop of Canterbury, Archbishop of York, then a diocese under a bishop, then the archdeaconry, the deanery, the parish, the rector, and the vicar. This was a clergy–laity model, where the clergy did most of the ministry and the laity, often being lazy, watched.

In varying degrees, Lutheran and Methodist Churches retained similar hierarchical features.

Puritans and Presbyterians adopted features of Calvin's congregation model. Puritans endeavored to purify the Anglican Church from within. Their emphasis was on the non-clergy or "laity."

U.S. Secretary of the Navy George Bancroft wrote in *The History of the United States,* 1834:

> Puritanism exalted the laity.

Presbyterian Church did not try to purify the Anglican Church. Each congregation was independent, with no bishops overseeing them. In Scotland, notably during persecutions, small covenant groups were called "conventicles," coming from Jesus, who said in Matthew 18:20 (NKJV), "For where two or three are gathered together in my name, there am I in the midst of them." This was the origin of the Scottish name "covenanters."

Presbyterian congregations were led by a pastor with elders or presbyters. Presbyters from the congregations in that area would meet together in synods. *Synod* is the Greek word for "meeting" or "assembly," equivalent to the Latin word "council." *Synagogue* in Hebrew means "meeting place." Presbyters representing their churches would enter into covenant.

Montesquieu, in *The Spirit of the Laws*, 1748, compared Lutheran and Calvinist structures:

> In the countries themselves where the Protestant religion became established, the revolutions were made pursuant to the several plans of political government.
>
> Luther having great princes on his side ... an ecclesiastical authority ... while Calvin, having to do with people who lived under republican governments ...
>
> Each of these two religions was believed to be perfect; the Calvinist judging his most conformable to what Christ had said, and the Lutheran to what the Apostles had practiced.

Others churches adapted Calvinist covenant features, such as:

• in England, by Pilgrims, Baptists, Congregationalists, Brownists, Levellers, Diggers, Enthusiasts, Quakers, and others;

• in the Netherlands by Dutch Reformed; and

• in Germany and other areas of Europe by Anabaptists, Mennonites, Amish, Huterites, United Brethren, and others.

With variations, members were only those

drawn by the Holy Spirit to be there. Each member was expected to have a personal relationship with God and regularly read through the Bible. Each member had individual rights and free choice. Elders and pastors were elected by the voice of the majority rather than appointed by a bishop.

These congregations were even more independent, not only separating from bishops but from agreements in synods with other churches. This gave rise to their nickname "separatists," "non-conformists," or "dissenters."

George Bancroft detailed John Calvin's influence, through the Puritans, on American political thought in *The History of the United States* (Vol. 1, 1834, Boston: Little Brown, 1856):

> The church existed independent of its pastor, who owed his office to its free choice; the will of the majority was its law; and each one of the brethren possessed equal rights with the elders.
>
> The right, exercised by each congregation, of electing its own ministers was in itself a moral revolution; religion was now with the people, not over the people. Puritanism exalted the laity ...
>
> Puritanism constituted not the Christian clergy, but the Christian people, the interpreter of the divine will. The voice of the majority was the voice

of God; and the issue of Puritanism was popular sovereignty ...

Puritanism was a life-giving spirit ... The people did not attempt to convert others, but to protect themselves; they never punished opinion as such; they never attempted to torture or terrify men into orthodoxy.

Lingyu Kong wrote in the article "George Bancroft's Transcendental View of American History under the Influence of Puritan Tradition" (*International Journal of Business and Social Science* Vol. 12, No. 10, October 2021):

The fruit of the Puritan seed, according to Bancroft, included such American fundamental thinking as popular sovereignty, or rule by the people, and liberty of conscience.

Finally, at the opposite end of the spectrum from hierarchical were the Quakers. They had no bishops, no presbyters, and often, no pastors or ministers. Everyone was equal, men, women, white, black. They were just a Society of Friends.

# BELIEVERS DO WORK OF THE MINISTRY

In covenant congregations, the pastor's role

was helping each person have their own personal relationship with God the Father through Jesus Christ who died on the cross to pay for their sins, and then coach them to become mature Christians.

Emphasis was placed on literacy and for each believer to develop the habits of reading through the Bible themselves, praying daily, and then plugging into the body and doing something, because everything that is alive takes in and gives out; for every muscle to grow it must be exercised.

A believer is not just to watch someone do the ministry and give a good message. They have to personally be involved.

Find an area of ministry and volunteer: nursery, junior high, Sunday school, outreach, seniors, benevolence, or community involvement. Then, filled with the Holy Spirit and the Word of God, the Lord will use them to meet the need.

In the process they will grow spiritually. "He that is faithful in that which is least is faithful also in much" (Luke 16:10, NKJV).

In this scenario, the pastors' role is to train church members to do the work of the ministry. "Christ gave some to be ... pastors and teachers, for the equipping of the saints for the work of ministry, for the edifying of the body of Christ" (Ephesians 4:11–12, NKJV).

Water seeks its own level. If a person with a need, be it spiritual, emotional, financial or physical, is around believers who are sensitive to the leading of the Holy Spirit, they will be drawn to minister to that person, and feel the joy of the Lord for letting Him use them.

Much ministry takes place in the church lobby, where people minister to each other. An older lady may see a young mother struggling and goes over and offers to help. An older man may encourage a young husband to meet with the guys for coffee and Bible study to learn how to be a godly husband.

This was one reason the COVID-19 response was problematic – it changed church structure from congregational to hierarchical. Believers either social-distance from each other or stopped gathering together, opting to hear a good sermon in the isolation of their home on a TV or computer.

They were taking in but not giving out. Their relationship with God was through a screen. They were taking in a good sermon, but there was no one around to minister to. One cannot witness to a pillow.

# ENGLISH SEPARATIST BAPTISTS

John Smyth, Thomas Helwys, and John Murton are considered the founders of the first

Baptist Church in 1612. John Murton was arrested by the Anglican government which put him in the Newgate Prison, where he died in 1626. Murton stated:

> No man ought to be persecuted for his religion ... The ... practices of Christ and his disciples, teaches no such thing as compelling men by persecutions and afflictions to obey the gospel.

Another Baptist founder who died in the Newgate Prison was Helwys, who wrote in 1612:

> The King is a mortal man, and not God, therefore he hath no power over the mortal soul of his subjects to make laws and ordinances for them and to set spiritual Lords over them ...

> If the King's people obey all humane laws made by the King, our lord the King can require no more ...

> For men's religion to God is betwixt God and themselves; the King shall not answer for it, neither may the King be judge between God and man.

A later Baptist preacher, John Leland, wrote in *Rights of Conscience Inalienable*, 1791:

> Every man must give account of himself to God, and therefore every man ought to be at liberty to serve God in a way that he can best reconcile to his conscience.

> If government can answer for individuals at the day of judgment, let men be controlled by it in religious matters; otherwise, let men be free.

Roger Williams, the Baptist founder of Rhode Island, wrote in *Plea for Religious Liberty,* 1644:

> The doctrine of persecution for cause of conscience is most contrary to the doctrine of Christ Jesus the Prince of Peace ...

> God requireth not a uniformity of religion to be enacted and enforced in any civil state ...

> Enforced uniformity (sooner or later) is the greatest occasion of civil war, ravishing of conscience, persecution of Christ Jesus in his servants, and of the hypocrisy and destruction of millions of souls.

# PILGRIMS FLED TO HOLLAND

King Charles I insisted on the hierarchical church structure with him at the top, maintaining control through bishops, as he exclaimed "no bishop, no king." He threatened to persecute Pilgrims, Puritans, dissenters and other nonconformists, saying:

> I will make them conform themselves or I will harry them out of the land.

John Robinson's church branched off of John Smyth's Baptist Church and in 1608, fled from Scrooby, England, to Holland, the most tolerant country in Europe. They settled in Leiden, just twenty-five miles from Amsterdam.

Leiden had an annual Day of Thanksgiving commemorating the ending of the bloody "Spanish Fury" of 1572. William the Silent, Prince of Orange, had rescued the city from the Spanish Fury. He ingeniously broke the dykes holding the sea water back and it flooded the countryside around Leiden, drowning the Spanish who were laying siege.

In 1575, William the Silent founded the University of Leiden. Among the courses taught were the study of Hebrew, Aramaic and Syriac. A rabbi reportedly taught in Leiden, as well as Pilgrim leader William Brewster.

There, Pilgrims would have encountered a thriving community of Jews who had fled from Spain to Portugal and then to the Netherlands. Jews celebrated an annual Feast of Thanksgiving called Tabernacles or Sukkot.

Pilgrims who fled from the king in England with their covenant government particularly identified with the Israelites who fled from the pharaoh in Egypt and set up a covenant government.

Evidence that the Pilgrims admired Jewish

heritage can be seen in Pilgrim Governor William Bradford's statement in *Of Plymouth Plantation*:

> Though I am grown aged, yet I have had a longing desire, to see with my own eyes, something of the most ancient language, and holy tongue, in which the Law, and oracles of God were writ; and in which God, and angels, spoke to the holy patriarchs, of old time; and what names were given to things, from the creation.

> And though I cannot attain to much herein, yet I am refreshed, to have seen some glimpse hereof; (as Moses saw the Land of Canaan afar off) my aim and desire is, to see how the words, and phrases lay in the holy text; and to discern somewhat of the same for my own content.

Governor Bradford's gravestone at Burial Hill in Plymouth, Massachusetts, had a Hebrew phrase inscribed on it:

> Under this stone rests the ashes of William Bradford, a zealous Puritan, and sincere Christian Governor of Plymouth Colony from 1621 to 1657, aged 69, except 5 years, which he declined. [Hebrew phrase] "Let the right hand of the Lord awake."

# MAYFLOWER

When Spain threatened to attack Holland, the Pilgrims decided to sail again. In 1620, the Pilgrims sailed from Holland to England and then set sail on the *Mayflower* to Virginia. Though Virginia was Anglican, they thought that the distance of 3,000 miles of ocean would allow them to practice their faith unnoticed.

Providentially, they were caught in a storm and got blown off course to the shores of Cape Cod, Massachusetts. They tried sailing south but almost sank in a storm.

The captain of the *Mayflower*, Christopher Jones, told everyone to get off the boat, but they had a question — who would be in charge. There was no king appointed person in their little boat.

At the time, nearly the whole world was ruled by kings, kaisers, khans, tsars, sultans, emperors, maharajas, chieftains, and stadtholders, but there was no king appointed person on the *Mayflower*.

The Pilgrims did not want to be lawless so they did something unique. They gave themselves the authority to start a government. It is called the *Mayflower Compact*. The word compact means covenant.

> We ... having undertaken for the Glory of God, and advancement of the Christian Faith ... plant the first colony

*Silence Equals Consent*

in the northern parts of Virginia ...

In the presence of God and one another, covenant and combine ourselves together into a civil body politic ... and ... enact ... just and equal laws ... as shall be thought most meet ... unto which we promise all due submission.

This was a church group of 102 people, which included some "strangers," who covenanted themselves "into a civil body politic." Imagine that, a church group forming itself into a political group.

It was a polarity change in the flow of power on planet Earth. Separatist Pilgrims fled from the king's top-down government and set up a bottom-up government.

Instead of hierarchical, it was congregational. In the womb of the *Mayflower* was conceived the child of self-government.

It was like a change from a dead pyramid with a king sending down mandates, to a living tree, where every root, even the tiniest capillary roots, participate in drawing up water and nutrients to keep the tree alive.

It is the difference between the divine right of kings — do what I say or I will kill you — and a self-governing "we the people" who rule ourselves through morals and virtue.

The Pilgrims, followed by the Puritans, brought

with them their covenant plan of government.

Os Guinness explained June 5, 2017:

> Covenantal ideas in England were the lost cause ... but the lost cause became the winning cause in New England and covenant shaped constitutionalism ...
>
> The American Constitution is a nationalized, secularized form of covenant ... Covenant lies behind constitution.

Puritans founded Harvard and taught the covenant plan, setting America on the path of self-government which culminated in the U.S. Constitution.

Franklin D. Roosevelt stated October 28, 1936:

> Rulers ... increased their power over the common men.
>
> The seamen they sent to find gold found instead the way of escape for the common man from those rulers ...
>
> What they found over the Western horizon was not the silk and jewels of Cathay [China) but MANKIND'S SECOND CHANCE – a chance to create a new world after he had almost spoiled an old one ...
>
> The Almighty seems purposefully to have withheld that SECOND CHANCE until the time when men would most need and appreciate liberty ...

> Those who came ... had courage ...
> to abandon language and relatives ...
> to start ... without influence, without
> money ...
>
> Perhaps Providence did prepare this
> American continent to be a place of the
> SECOND CHANCE.

Poet Ralph Waldo Emerson wrote in *The Atlantic Magazine*, April 1862:

> America is another word for
> opportunity. Our whole history appears
> like a last effort of the Divine Providence
> in behalf of the human race.

# CHURCH BODY KNIT TOGETHER

Sir Edwin Sandy was a generous member of Parliament who lent the Pilgrims 300 pounds, at no interest, to finance their journey. Pastor John Robinson wrote to him in 1617 of the Pilgrims:

> We are knit together as a body
> in a most strict and sacred bond and
> covenant of the Lord ... whereof we do
> hold ourselves straightly tied to all care
> of each other's good.

Puritan founder of Massachusetts John Winthrop is credited with writing "A Model of Christian Charity," stating:

This love among Christians is a real thing ... We are knit together by this bond of love. We must make one another's condition our own, rejoice together, mourn together, labor, and suffer together. We shall find that the God of Israel is among us.

Prime Minister Margaret Thatcher explained in an interview with Joseph A. Cannon, February 5, 1996, (*Human Events*) that the founders felt a responsibility to God to care for each other:

If you accept freedom, you've got to have principles about the responsibility. You can't do this without a biblical foundation.

Your Founding Fathers came over with that. They came over with the doctrines of the New Testament as well as the Old. They looked after one another, not only as a matter of necessity, but as a matter of duty to their God.

There is no other country in the world which started that way.

This was not Marxist socialism where the state is god; where a person gets their "rights" from the state and is accountable to the state; where the state involuntarily takes away private possessions and redistributes them to their supporters.

What America's founders envisioned was individuals having private property, in voluntary acts of love, caring for each other.

&

# DEMOCRACY IN ATHENS: EKKLESIA

**K**ings have "subjects" who are subjected to the king's will. Democracies and republics have citizens. The word "citizen" is Greek, meaning co-sovereign, co-ruler co-king.

What is the difference between a republic and democracy?

The word democracy has two main meanings. The first is a general reference to a popular form of government where the population is involved in ruling itself. The second is a functional form of government, like the city–state of Athens.

The word "demos" means "people" and "cracy" means "rule." In a democracy the people rule. In Athens, every citizen was expected to be at every meeting everyday to talk about every issue. It was very time consuming. If a citizen did not keep up with what was being talked about, or neglected being involved, they were called an *idiotes*.

A republic is where citizens take care of their families and farms, and have someone in their place go to the marketplace every day to talk politics. That person is called a "representative." An easy way to remember is — both words "republic" and "representative" begin with the letters "rep." A republican form of government is a representative form of government.

In democracies, citizens rule directly, but in republics, citizens rule indirectly.

In Athens, there were 6,000 citizens, who would be called out of their homes to the *agora* marketplace where they collectively assembled as the *ekklesia* — "*ek*" means "out of" and "*klesia*" means "called."

Assembled citizens participated in deliberating and giving consent to what needed to be done to protect and provide for the city and who was to be given responsibility for various tasks.

When Jesus said, "upon this rock I will build my church" (Matthew 16:18), the word He used for church was *ekklesia*, meaning congregation or assembly, in other words the Body of Christ.

Every believer is involved in the Body, as the Apostle Paul wrote in I Corinthians 12:12–26 (NIV):

> The body is a unit, though it is composed of many parts ... So it is with Christ .... For in one Spirit we were all baptized into one body ...
>
> If the foot should say, "Because I am not a hand, I do not belong to the

body," that would not make it any less a part of the body. And if the ear should say, "Because I am not an eye, I do not belong to the body," that would not make it any less a part of the body ...

God has arranged the members of the body, every one of them, according to His design ...

There should be no division in the body, but that its members should have mutual concern for one another. If one part suffers, every part suffers with it; if one part is honored, every part rejoices with it.

Historian James F. Cooper, Jr., explained that Puritans had "local self-government, and, especially, extensive lay participation."

# NEW ENGLAND PASTORS FOUNDED CITIES

After King James I died, his son, Charles I, turned up the heat. He persecuted not just Separatist Pilgrims but also Puritans. This resulted in the Great Puritan Migration of 1630–1640.

Some 20,000 Puritans abandoned England and fled to the New England colonies of

Massachusetts, Connecticut, Rhode Island, New Hampshire, and Maine. They carried with them an estimated one-fifth of the wealth of England.

Those that did not leave were caught up in the English Civil War.

In New England, Puritans with their pastors founded cities. Pastor Thomas Hooker and his church founded Hartford, Connecticut in 1636, and the first Congregational church in America;

Pastor Roger Williams and his church founded Providence, Rhode Island in 1636, and the first Baptist church in America;

Pastor John Wheelwright and his church founded Exeter, New Hampshire in 1638; and

Pastor John Lothropp and his church founded Barnstable, Massachusetts 1639.

New England was a little greenhouse on planet Earth. At a time when the world was ruled by kings, khans, tsars, sultans, Emperors, maharajas, chieftains and stadtholders, in New England were pastors and churches founding cities, and creating the laws for those cities.

# PASTOR THOMAS HOOKER FOUNDED HARTFORD

Hartford, Connecticut, is worth examining

*Silence Equals Consent*

in depth. In 1636, Reverend Thomas Hooker had a conflict with Boston's Puritan Reverend John Cotton over who was allowed to vote in elections: Cotton insisted only Puritans could vote; whereas Hooker said anyone who was a Christian should be allowed to vote.

This led Hooker to lead his "covenant" congregation in 1636 from Massachusetts, through the wilderness, to found the city of Hartford, Connecticut.

Settlers soon asked Reverend Hooker if he would preach a sermon on how they should set up their government. Nearly a century before Europe's "Age of Enlightenment," Reverend Hooker preached a sermon, May 31, 1638, explaining:

> The foundation of authority is laid
> in the free *consent of the people.*

This phrase was later reflected in the Declaration of Independence:

> Government from the *consent of the governed.*

This was radically different from Europe where kings did not ask the people for their consent. They claimed to be "divinely appointed" and ruled through fear, having armies to force their subjects to obey.

The first use of paper ballots in America was in church. The Massachusetts Bay Colony used paper ballots in 1629 to select a pastor for the Salem Church.

Since the goal was God's will, instead of casting lots, church members fasted and prayed, then cast their ballots, thus participating in having God's will be done through them.

The belief was, that God had preordained someone to be their pastor and church members were simply to recognize the one God had chosen.

Being chosen by God was called being "the elect." I Peter 1:1–2 (NIV):

> Peter, an apostle of Jesus Christ, to God's elect.

Paul wrote in Colossians 3:12:

> As the elect of God, holy and beloved, put on tender mercies.

Second Timothy 2:10:

> I endure all things for the sake of the elect.

Mark 13:20 (ASV) described the last days:

> And except that the Lord had shortened those days, no flesh should be saved: but for the sake of the elect, whom he hath chosen, he hath shortened the days.

The process of putting down the name of God's "elect" was called an "election."

Rev. Hooker explained:

> The privilege of election ... belongs to *the people* ... according to the blessed

will and law of God.

This is reflected in the U.S. Constitution: "We, *the People*."

President Calvin Coolidge explained how elections came from congregational churches:

> We have the principle of the consent of the governed stated by Reverend Thomas Hooker as early as 1638 ...

Coolidge continued:

> Placing every man on a plane where he acknowledged no superiors, where no one possessed any right to rule over him, he must inevitably choose his own rulers through a system of self-government ...
>
> In those days such doctrines would scarcely have been permitted to flourish and spread in any other country.

Coolidge stated April 19, 1926:

> Election day in the olden times was generally considered more or less sacred.

Coolidge added, November 3, 1924:

> I therefore urge upon all the voters of our country ... that they assemble tomorrow at their respective voting places in the exercise of the high office of American citizenship, that they approach the ballot box in the spirit that they would approach a sacrament,

and ... make their choice of public officers solely in the light of their own conscience.

When an election is so held, when a choice is so made, it ... sustains the belief that the voice of the people is the voice of God.

Hooker continued his sermon in 1638:

Deuteronomy 1:13 "Choose you wise men and understanding and known among your tribes and I will make them heads over you captains over thousands, captains over hundreds, fifties, tens" ...

The choice of public magistrates belongs unto the people by Gods own allowance ... They who have power to appoint officers and magistrates it is in their power also to set the bounds and limits of the power and places unto which they call them.

Hooker's sermon was written down and became the constitution for the colony, called *The Fundamental Orders of Connecticut*, used for nearly two centuries, from 1639 up until 1818.

*The Fundamental Orders of Connecticut* stated:

Where a people are gathered together the word of God requires that to maintain the peace ... there should be an orderly ... government established according to God ...

> The people ... conjoin ourselves to be as one public state or commonwealth ... to maintain and preserve the liberty and purity of the Gospel of our Lord Jesus which we now profess.

Who were "the people"? It was Pastor Hooker and his "covenant" congregation. Here again was a church group forming itself into a political group, similar to the Separatist Pilgrims with the *Mayflower Compact:* "We ... covenant ... ourselves together into a civil body politic."

It is noteworthy that they picked the form of government which would best "preserve the liberty and purity of the Gospel of our Lord Jesus."

The ideas proposed in Hooker's sermon were revolutionary as for most of the world, the foundation of authority was the will of a divinely–appointed king, emperor, czar, sultan, maharaja, or chieftain. Nowhere in *The Fundamental Orders* is any acknowledgment made to the king as in other charters, ie.: "our dread Sovereign"; "our gracious Lord the King."

Instead of the top-down government, like a pyramid, with a "divinely–appointed" king ruling through fear, it was a bottom-up government, like the roots of a tree, drawing nourishment from the virtuous involvement of every citizen.

Settlers had fled from Europe where kings

would burn people at the stake for not believing the way they did.

New England pastors understood that since Jesus never forced anyone to follow him, they could not either. The Kingdom of God was not to be forced top-down by a theocratic king.

The only way for it to happen was if the majority of people held godly values and willingly voted for representatives holding those same values. Then laws would be passed reflecting those values, and the values of the Kingdom of God could come, voluntarily, from the bottom-up.

Psalm 110:3 stated: "Thy people shall be willing in the day of Thy power."

*The Fundamental Orders* were used in Connecticut until 1818, serving as a blueprint for other New England colonies and eventually the United States Constitution.

*The Fundamental Orders of Connecticut* were described by Historian John Fiske in his book *Beginnings of New England, Cambridge*, 1889:

> The first written constitution known to history that created a government. It marked the beginnings of American democracy, of which Thomas Hooker deserves more than any other man to be called the father.
>
> The government of the United States today is in lineal descent more nearly related to that of Connecticut than to

that of any of the other thirteen colonies.

Connecticut was designated "The Constitution State" in 1959.

A statue of Reverend Thomas Hooker holding a Bible stands prominently at the Connecticut State Capitol, with the inscription on the base:

> Leading his people through the wilderness, he founded Hartford in June of 1636. On this site he preached the sermon which inspired The Fundamental Orders. It was the first written Constitution that created a government.

A marker on the back of Center Church next to Hartford's Ancient Burial Grounds, reads:

> Thomas Hooker 1586–1657 • A Leader of the Founders of this Commonwealth • A Preacher of Persuasive Power who Based All Civil Authority on the Free Consent of the People • This tablet is placed near the site of his burial by The Connecticut Society of The Colonial Dames of America. A.D. 1915."

A plaque erected in Hartford by the Daughters of the American Revolution reads:

> In 1636, The Church in Newtown, Massachusetts, Thomas Hooker, Minister, was transplanted to this locality, called Meeting House Yard, Old State House Square, City Hall Square.

Near this site on May 31, 1638, Thomas Hooker preached his Famous Sermon: "The Foundation of Authority is Laid In the Free Consent of the People."

Near this site on January 14, 1639, representatives of the three river towns adopted *The Fundamental Orders Of Connecticut,* "The first written constitution known to history that created a government."

A historical marker in England reads:

Thomas Hooker 1586–1647, Curate of St. Mary's Church, Chelmsford and Town Lecturer 1626–1629, Founder of the State of Connecticut 1636, "Father of American Democracy."

Another marker reads:

Hinckley & Bosworth Borough Council, Thomas Hooker, 1586–1647, Puritan Clergyman, Pupil of this School, Reputed Father of "American Democracy."

A plaque in Cambridge, Massachusetts, reads:

Here Stood The Original Meeting House of the First Church in Cambridge. Built in 1632 and the center of the Civic and Religious Life of the Town. Here Ministered 1633–1636 Thomas Hooker – A Peerless Leader of New England Thought and Life in both Church and State.

Hartford's Traveler's Square has a bronze

*Silence Equals Consent*

statue of Connecticut's first settlers and a plaque which reads:

> In June of 1635, about one hundred members of Thomas Hooker's congregation arrived safely in this vicinity with one hundred and sixty cattle.
>
> They followed old Indian trails from Massachusetts Bay Colony to the Connecticut River to build a community.
>
> Here they established the form of government upon which the present Constitution of the United States is modeled.

This is a significant acknowledgment, that their "covenant" congregational church government became their colonial government which became the U.S. Constitution. The word "federal" is from the Latin word *foedus* which means "covenant."

A commentary on this was written by Dr. Charles Hull Wolfe, who had been a Marxist till he changed his views after conducting an independent study of American economics. He helped found and was the first executive director of The Plymouth Rock Foundation.

Dr. Wolfe, with Dr. D. James Kennedy, wrote "Restoring the Real Meaning of Thanksgiving," 1989:

> When the brilliant Rev. Thomas Hooker left Boston and settled in Hartford, he promptly called for three

Connecticut towns to join together in forming a colony.

Hooker followed the Pilgrim pattern and led the people of Connecticut in framing a written compact for civil self-government rooted in Mosaic tradition.

He used as his text, "Take you wise men, and understanding, and known among your tribes, and I will make them rulers over you." (Deuteronomy 1:13).

Hooker preached a scholarly sermon that guided the men of Connecticut in framing the *Fundamental Orders of Connecticut* in 1639, commonly called "the world's first complete written constitution," though, in fact, Plymouth had framed a complete constitutional charter, the Pilgrim Code of Law, three years before.

*The Fundamental Orders of Connecticut* added:

According to the truth of the said Gospel ... our civil affairs to be guided and governed according to such Laws, Rules, Orders and Decrees as shall be made ...

The Governor ... shall have the power to administer justice according to the Laws here established, and for want thereof, according to the Rule of the Word of God.

In New England, instead of separation of church and state, it was the pastors and their "covenant" churches that created the state!

How could someone say, "Pastor, do not preach on politics" when it is the pastor sermon that is their constitution. How could someone say "Church members should not be involved in politics" when all there was in Hartford were the church members. There were no non-church members there to be lazy and let them run things.

President Calvin Coolidge stated at the 150th anniversary of the Declaration of Independence, Philadelphia, July 5, 1926:

> The principles ... which went into the Declaration of Independence ... are found in ... the sermons ... of the early colonial clergy who were earnestly undertaking to instruct their congregations in the great mystery of how to live.
>
> They preached equality because they believed in the fatherhood of God and the brotherhood of man.
>
> They justified freedom by the text that we are all created in the divine image ...
>
> Placing every man on a plane where he acknowledged no superiors, where no one possessed any right to rule over him, he must inevitably choose his own rulers through a system of self-government ...
>
> In order that they might have freedom to express these thoughts and opportunity to put them into action, whole

congregations with their pastors migrated to the colonies.

Romans 13:1 states:

> Let everyone be subject to the governing authorities, for there is no authority except that which God has established.

In other countries the authority was the king. A "king," is defined in *Webster's 1828 Dictionary*:

> The chief or sovereign of a nation; a man invested with supreme authority over a nation, tribe or country; a monarch. Kings are absolute.

In America, God allowed the founders to establish a republic where, instead of a single man being the supreme authority, the people are the supreme authority.

In a monarchy, subjects submit to the king, but in a republic the citizens ARE the king. Subjects "obey," whereas citizens "give consent." When citizens "pledge allegiance to the flag and to the republic," they are pledging allegiance to being in charge of themselves. When someone protests the flag, they are saying I don't want to be king anymore."

To reiterate, the King of England looked to the King Saul and beyond peritod of Bible history for his authority – the "divine right of kings" but in contrast, the colonial founders of America looked to the pre-King Saul period of Bible history, the four hundred year period of the Hebrew Republic, where millions of people were taught the Law and were personally accountable to God to follow it.

# THE MEETING HOUSE

In each New England city there was one main building called a meeting house. This is where the pastor would teach the Bible and where they would gather together to do their city business.

The word "synagogue" means "meeting house." That is where the rabbi would teach the Law and where they would gather together to do their city business. Why build a separate building just to talk about a different topic? Each citizen was involved in affairs of both church and state.

When the Revolutionary War started, the British sent over a military governor, Thomas Gage. He outlawed meeting houses saying "Democracy is too prevalent in America." His attitude was, the people do not need to meet and give their consent. The people are just supposed to obey government mandates.

The word "politics" comes from the word "polis" which means "city" – like Minneapolis and Indianapolis. "Politics" is simply "the business of the city." This was an advancement over the

European tradition of Thomistic "subsidiarity," namely, that whenever possible, civic problems should be solved at the most local level, allowing parishes a limited degree of autonomy.

To repeat for emphasis, Calvin Coolidge stated at the 150th anniversary of the Declaration of Independence, July 5, 1926:

> The principles ... which went into the Declaration of Independence ... are found in ... the sermons ... of the early colonial clergy ... They preached equality because they believed in the fatherhood of God and the brotherhood of man.

Kings did not necessarily believe in "equality" or the "brotherhood of man." They believed they were created extra special, a superior royal class. It was called "the divine right of kings."

Coolidge continued describing colonial churches:

> Placing every man on a plane where he acknowledged no superiors, where no one possessed any right to rule over him, he must inevitably choose his own rulers through a system of self-government ...
>
> In those days such doctrines would scarcely have been permitted to flourish and spread in any other country ...
>
> In order that they might have freedom to express these thoughts and

opportunity to put them into action, whole congregations with their pastors migrated to the colonies.

Coolidge added:

> Rev. Thomas Hooker of Connecticut as early as 1638, when he said in a sermon before the General Court that: "The foundation of authority is laid in the free consent of the people ... The choice of public magistrates belongs unto the people by God's own allowance."

> This doctrine found wide acceptance among the nonconformist clergy who later made up the Congregational Church.

# PASTOR JOHN WISE

Calvin Coolidge continued his address, July 5, 1926, by explaining the contribution of another pastor, Rev. John Wise:

> The great apostle of this movement was the Rev. John Wise of Massachusetts.

> He was one of the leaders of the revolt against the royal governor Andros in 1687, for which he suffered imprisonment ...

> His works were reprinted in 1772 and have been declared to have been nothing less than a textbook of liberty for our Revolutionary fathers ...

That these ideas were prevalent in Virginia is further revealed by the Declaration of Rights, which was prepared by George Mason and presented to the general assembly on May 27, 1776.

This document asserted popular sovereignty and inherent natural rights, but confined the doctrine of equality to the assertion that 'All men are created equally free and independent.'

It can scarcely be imagined that Jefferson was unacquainted with what had been done in his own Commonwealth of Virginia when he took up the task of drafting the Declaration of Independence ...

These thoughts can very largely be traced back to what Rev. John Wise was writing in 1710. He said ... "Democracy is Christ's government in church and state."

Here was the doctrine of equality, popular sovereignty, and the substance of the theory of inalienable rights clearly asserted by Wise at the opening of the eighteenth century, just as we have the principle of the consent of the governed stated by Hooker as early as 1638.

When we take all these circumstances into consideration, it is but natural that the first paragraph of the Declaration of Independence should open with a reference to Nature's God and should close in the final paragraphs with an appeal to the Supreme Judge of the world and an assertion of a firm reliance on Divine Providence ...

In its main feature the Declaration of Independence is a great spiritual document ...

Equality, liberty, popular sovereignty, the rights of man – these are not elements which we can see and touch ... They have their source and their roots in the religious convictions ...

Unless the faith of the American in these religious convictions is to endure, the principles of our Declaration will perish. We cannot continue to enjoy the result if we neglect and abandon the cause ...

If anyone wishes to deny their truth ... the only direction in which he can proceed ... is ... backward toward the time when there was no equality, no rights of the individual, no rule of the people ...

The duly authorized expression of the will of the people has a divine sanction ... The ultimate sanction of law rests on the righteous authority of the Almighty ... It was in the contemplation of these truths that the fathers made their Declaration and adopted their Constitution ...

Their intellectual life centered around the meeting–house. They were intent upon religious worship ... While scantily provided with other literature, there was a wide acquaintance with the Scriptures ...

We live in an age of science and of abounding accumulation of material things. These did not create the Declaration. Our Declaration created them. The things of the spirit come first.

Unless we cling to that, all our material prosperity, overwhelming though it may appear, will turn to a barren sceptre in our grasp ... We must not sink into a pagan materialism.

We must cultivate the reverence which they had for the things that are holy. We must follow the spiritual and moral leadership which they showed.

We must keep replenished, that they may glow with a more compelling flame, the altar fires before which they worshiped.

Because of the activism of Rev. John Wise, his hometown of Ipswich, Massachusetts, calls itself "The Birthplace of American Independence."

Through his wife, Rev. John Wise was a great-uncle of John Adams. Wise stated in a sermon at Chebacco Parish of Ipswich (Essex), circa 1700:

The first human subject and original of civil power is the people ... and when they are free, they may set up what species of government they please. The end of all good government is ... the good of every man in all his rights, his life, liberty, estate.

Alexis de Tocqueville wrote in *Democracy in America* (1835; 1840):

> Americans ... brought with them ... a form of Christianity which I cannot better describe than by styling it a democratic and republican religion ...

> From the earliest settlement of the emigrants, politics and religion contracted an alliance which has never been dissolved.

∽

# WILLIAM PENN AND THE QUAKERS

George Fox was born in England in 1624. He went even further than Puritans in rejecting state-sponsored Anglican ritualism and joined a separatist Puritan sect called Seekers.

During the English Commonwealth, 1649–1660, Fox founded the Quakers. It was on the complete other end of the spectrum from a hierarchical church structure. Emphasizing "the priesthood of the believer" they did not even have a pastor. It was just a "Society of Friends."

Fox spoke of the inspiration or "inner light" of the Holy Spirit giving him insights or "openings," as in Luke 24:45 "Then *opened* He their understanding, that they might understand the scriptures." George Fox wrote in his *Journal*:

These things I did not see by the help of man, nor by the letter, though they are written in the letter, but I saw them in the light of the Lord Jesus Christ, and by his immediate Spirit and powers, as did the holy men of God, by whom the Holy Scriptures were written.

One of the individuals influenced by the Quakers was William Penn.

William Penn's father was a commander in the British navy. During the English Commonwealth under Oliver Cromwell, Penn's father was suspected of corresponding with the exiled Charles II. He was arrested and imprisoned in the Tower of London. Fortunately for him, he was soon released.

At this time, a Quaker missionary named Thomas Loe visited the Penn estate in Ireland and explained to 15-year-old William that religion was more than a plan or doctrine approved by the government, it was a personal relationship with the indwelling of the Holy Spirit.

Young Penn later recalled that it was during this time that: "... the Lord visited me and gave me divine Impressions of Himself."

In the next seven years, Penn attended the coronation of King Charles II with his father, and became a student at the prestigious Oxford University.

It caused a stir when William was expelled from Oxford for not attending Anglican chapel and for criticizing the rituals. He was sent by his father to be educated in Europe.

Upon return he intended to follow his father's footstep with a military career, helping to subdue an Irish Catholic revolt, and serving as an aid to his father in a war against the Dutch.

There was the Great Plague of London, 1665, then the Great Fire of London, 1666, burning a quarter of the city. When his father became ill, young Penn went back to Ireland in order to oversee the family estate.

At age 22, Penn visited a Quaker meeting in Cork, Ireland. By chance, he became reacquainted with Thomas Loe. Suddenly the unauthorized meeting was raided by the police.

Instead of distancing himself from the Quakers, Penn surprised everyone by proclaiming he was one. Trained as a lawyer, Penn argued at court that since the Quakers had no political agenda, like the Puritans, they should not be subject to laws restricting religious meetings.

His family name got him out of jail, but when his father, the Admiral, heard of it, he immediately summoned him to London. His father severely scolded him as his actions were jeopardizing his father's position at the Royal Court.

His father warned him that by rejecting state-sponsored Anglican doctrine he was on a collision course with the Crown, but young Penn would not abandon his convictions. Enraged, his father kicked him out and threatened to disinherit him, but could not bring himself to do it.

With no place to go, Penn lived with the Quakers. He traveled with Quaker Josiah Coale, who had just returned to England from America.

It was Coale who suggested the idea to Penn of setting up a utopian colony in America. Penn then met and traveled with Quaker founder George Fox.

In 1668, Penn was imprisoned in the Tower of London, where he wrote "No Cross, No Crown":

> Christ's cross is Christ's way to Christ's crown ... It is a false notion that they may be children of God while in a state of disobedience to his holy commandments, and disciples of Jesus though they revolt from his cross.

He wrote in *England's Present Interest Considered*, 1675:

> Force makes hypocrites, 'tis persuasion only that makes converts.

Penn was arrested several more times, and his father interceded for his release. Realizing he was championing the cause of religious liberty, Penn wrote to his father: "I intreat thee not to purchase my liberty."

Nevertheless, the dying father petitioned King Charles II to be considerate of young Penn. After the father's death, and after Penn was arrested several more times, he took his inheritance and requested Charles II allow him to purchase land in West Jersey for the Quakers to immigrate to.

Charles II surprised Penn in 1682 by giving him 45,000 square miles in America, naming the land after his father, Admiral Penn –Pennsylvania.

Even though he was given the land from the King, William Penn insisted on paying the Indians a fair price for land for colonists to settle upon.

As Quakers were known for being non-violent and tolerant, Penn desired for the colony to be a "holy experiment" of Christians of different denominations living together.

In 1750, a Quaker in Pennsylvania, Anthony Benezet, began a school to teach black children. He advocated for Indian Natives and started the first school for girls in America in 1754. In 1758, at the yearly meeting, Benezet led Quakers to officially oppose slavery.

# PROTESTANTISM

Following the Reformation, 1517, and the Peace of Augsburg, 1555, different kings chose different denominations for their kingdoms. This resulted in millions migrating from one country to another simply for conscience sake.

Many of these Christian religious refugees fled Europe to settle colonies in America.

New York University Professor Emeritus Patricia Bonomi, in her article "The Middle Colonies as the Birthplace of American Religious Pluralism" wrote:

> The colonists were about 98 percent Protestant.

One to two percent of America's population at the time of the founding were Catholic, and one-tenth of a percent were Jewish.

The 56 signers of the Declaration were predominantly Protestant, with a notable exception being Charles Carroll of Maryland, a Catholic.

British Statesman Edmund Burke addressed Parliament, 1775:

> All Protestantism ... is a sort of dissent. But the religion most prevalent in our Northern Colonies is a refinement on the principle of resistance; it is the dissidence of dissent, and the protestantism of the Protestant religion.

Samuel Adams stated when he signed the Declaration of Independence, 1776:

> This day, I trust the reign of political protestantism will commence. We have

explored the temple of royalty, and found that the idol we have bowed down to, has eyes which see not, ears that hear not our prayers, and a heart like the nether millstone.

We have this day restored the Sovereign, to whom alone men ought to be obedient. He reigns in Heaven, and with a propitious eye beholds his subjects assuming that freedom of thought, and dignity of self-direction which He bestowed on them. From the rising to the setting sun, may His kingdom come

*Silence Equals Consent*

❧

# *OLD LIGHTS*

# PURITANS BECAME OLD LIGHTS

The 1600s saw the first wave of pastors and church members come to America, of which a significant amount were Calvinist Puritans. They were thrilled that believers could search the Scriptures and discover God's plan for their life, marriage, family, church and government.

One of the names for the Holy Spirit is *Paraclete*, which means Helper. The Holy Spirit illuminates the Scriptures so they give you direction, and then inspires you to follow the direction. In other words, the Holy Spirit helps you find God's will and do it.

> For we are his workmanship, created in Christ Jesus unto good works, which God has before ordained that we should walk in them (Ephesians 2:10).

> For it is God who works in you to will and to act in order to fulfill his good purpose (Philippians 2:13, NIV).

Puritans implemented God's government plan for people to rule themselves without a king – a covenant plan, borrowed from the ancient Hebrew Republic. Every person needed to agree to participate for it to work.

President Grover Cleveland commented on the

uniqueness of this on July 13, 1887:

> The sovereignty of sixty millions of free people, is, to my mind ... the working out ... of the divine right of man to govern himself and a manifestation of God's plan concerning the human race.

Many theological views were debated during this era, but suffice it to say that most colonial preachers believed it was their job to evangelize and leave it to God as to who would be saved.

Some took it a step further and examined deep polemic arguments regarding God's foreknowledge of who would be in heaven, the elect. After a century of Puritan teaching that God has it all planned, it became so plan-focused that it was *only* a plan.

Church members became reserved, passive, holding a "hands off" attitude regarding their part in spreading the Gospel. Calvinist teachings became less evangelistic and more doctrine-focused, formal, rigid, and spiritually dry. They got nicknamed "Old Lights."

It produced a *que sera sera* attitude – "whatever will be will be," similar to ancient Greece's three sister goddesses of destiny called "The Fates." Islam as well had a resignation belief of *al-qadar* that "what Allah willeth."

The same attitude of non-evangelism crept into Calvinists back in Scotland.

John Knox helped the Parliament recognize the Church of Scotland as "the national church of the Scottish people." It exercised spiritual jurisdiction over its own affairs independent of the king.

The title "minister" replaced the Anglican title "priest." Ministers were chosen by each congregation as stipulated in the First Book of Discipline, 1560, and the Second Book of Discipline, 1578.

After a few centuries, though, the Church of Scotland focused less on evangelism and began viewing itself an arm of the Scottish Parliament, due to the fact it had been recognized by an Act of Parliament. Like gravity, there was a pull toward hierarchy. Parliament claimed the right to appoint ministers rather than each local congregation.

A temporary compromise was the Veto Act of 1832, where a congregation could veto a government-appointed pastor. Finally, the Great Disruption of 1843 led independent–minded evangelicals to split and create the Free Church of Scotland. These evangelicals held Holy Fairs with open–air preaching that brought great revivals.

# DAVID BRAINERD
# EXPELLED FROM YALE

In response to the non-evangelical attitude of many Calvinists in New England, a revival swept through colonial America in the early 1700s called the Great Awakening.

Revivalist preachers taught that religion was more than a plan, as good as that plan may be. A person needed to have a personal experience with Jesus, and once they did, their life would change. Their lives would bear fruit of a new life.

These preachers and their followers were called New Lights. Soon a controversy began between the Old Lights and the New Lights.

Someone who was caught in the middle of this controversy was David Brainerd.

He was born in Haddam, Connecticut, April 20, 1718. His parents died while he was a young teenager. He attempted farming, but on July 12, 1739, he had an experience with God of "unspeakable glory" that gave him a desire to "seek first His Kingdom."

A Connecticut law forbade the appointment of ministers unless they graduated from Harvard, Yale or a European institution, so in 1740, Brainerd entered Yale.

His freshman year, he wrote:

> I was spending some time in prayer

and self-examination, when the Lord by His grace so shined into my heart that I enjoyed full assurance of His favor. Passages of God's Word opened to my soul with divine clearness, power, and sweetness ... with clear and certain evidence of its being the Word of God.

Old Light faculty professors at Harvard and Yale, were educated, established, formal, structured, rigid, and respected. They looked down upon the New Lights as less educated and unorganized, emotional and considered their enthusiastic Holy Spirit-led revivals as fanatic.

Great Awakening preaching spread onto college campuses causing students to focus on personal salvation. These preachers included: George Whitefield; Gilbert Tennent; Ebenezer Pemberton, Jonathan Edwards, and James Davenport.

David Brainerd described during his sophomore year at Yale that "a great and general awakening spread itself over the college" (David Wynbeck, *Beloved Yankee,* Eerdmans, 1965) .

He wrote: "I was much quickened and more abundantly engaged."

Wanting his classmates to know Jesus, he "visited each room in the college, and discussed freely and with great plainness."

Brainerd helped lead the "New Light"

movement at Yale. Rather than the dead religious formality of the "Old Lights," he wanted to exhibit "a living faith preached by a living preacher."

The Connecticut legislature were embarrassed to learn:

> Some undergraduate students have made it their practice, day and night, and sometimes for several days together, to go about in the town of New Haven as other towns, and before great numbers of people to teach and exhort, much after the same manner that ministers of the gospel do in their public preaching.

They urged the college to rein in these overzealous students, so in 1741, Yale trustees decreed:

> If any student of this College shall ... say, that the rector ... trustees or tutors are hypocrites, carnal or unconverted men, he shall for the first offense make a public confession in the hall, and for the second offense be expelled.

Brainerd was accused of saying that his tutor, Chauncey Whittelsey, "has no more grace than a chair." This resulted in David Brainerd being expelled from Yale. He later became a missionary to the Indians, traveling over 3,000 miles on horseback.

He often slept in cold, rainy woods till he became too ill to minister. Dying, he was taken in by Princeton President Jonathan Edwards, who wrote down his life story: *An Account of the Life of the Late Reverend Mr. David Brainerd*. It was published in 1749 and has never been out of print, inspiring millions.

Yale's Divinity School named a building "Brainerd Hall," the only building named after a student who had been expelled.

∽

# FRANKLIN CRITICIZED OLD LIGHTS

Benjamin Franklin criticized the Old Light Calvinists for being so focused on structure, doctrine and God's plan that they tended to neglect being evangelical, reaching the lost and being involved and doing good in the community.

In 1729, at the age of 23, he began publishing the *Pennsylvania Gazette*. He designed some of the very first political cartoons. He also published the sermons of the New Light Great Awakening preacher George Whitefield.

Franklin gives insight into the Old Light views versus the New Light views in his *Autobiography*:

> I had been religiously educated as a Presbyterian; and tho' some of the dogmas of that persuasion, such as

the eternal decrees of God, election, reprobation, etc., appeared to me unintelligible ... I early absented myself from the public assemblies of the sect ,.. I never was without some religious principles.

I never doubted, for instance, the existence of the Deity; that he made the world, and govern'd it by his Providence; that the most acceptable service of God was the doing good to man; that our souls are immortal; and that all crime will be punished, and virtue rewarded, either here or hereafter.

These I esteem'd the essentials ... found in all the religions we had in our country, I respected them all, tho' with different degrees ...

This respect to all, with an opinion that the worst had some good effects, induc'd me to avoid all discourse that might tend to lessen the good opinion another might have of his own religion ...

As our province increas'd in people, and new places of worship were continually wanted, and generally erected by voluntary contributions, my mite for such purpose, whatever might be the sect, was never refused ...

Franklin went on:

> Tho' I seldom attended any public worship, I had still an opinion of its propriety ...

> I regularly paid my annual subscription for the support of the only Presbyterian minister or meeting we had in Philadelphia. He us'd to visit me sometimes as a friend, and admonish me to attend his administrations, and I was now and then prevail'd on to do so, once for five Sundays successively.

> Had he been in my opinion a good preacher, perhaps I might have continued ... but his discourses were chiefly either polemic arguments, or explications of the peculiar doctrines of our sect, and were all to me very dry, uninteresting, and unedifying ... and I attended his preaching no more ...

> My conduct might be blameable, but I leave it, without attempting further to excuse it.

Franklin believed that Christians should not just hear sermons, but they should also be involved in doing things in their community, to affect society for the better. This included politics. Franklin wrote to Joseph Huey, On June 6, 1753:

> The worship of God is a duty; the hearing and reading of sermons may be useful; but, if men rest in hearing and

praying, as too many do, it is as if a tree should value itself on being watered and putting forth leaves, though it never produce any fruit.

# FRANKLIN DEFENDED PREACHER

At the age of 29, young Ben Franklin had been attending the First Presbyterian Church of Philadelphia. He wrote in his *Autobiography*:

> About the Year 1734, there arrived among us from Ireland, a young Presbyterian Preacher named Samuel Hemphill, who delivered with a good voice, and apparently extempore, most excellent discourses, which drew together considerable numbers of different persuasions, who join'd in admiring them.
>
> Among the rest I became one of his constant hearers, his sermons pleasing me, as they had little of the dogmatical kind, but inculcated strongly the practice of virtue, or what in the religious style are called good works ...
>
> Those however, of our Congregation, who considered themselves as orthodox Presbyterians, disapprov'd his doctrine, and were join'd by most of the old

Clergy, who arraign'd him of heterodoxy before the Synod, in order to have him silenc'd ...

I became his zealous partisan, and contributed all I could to raise a party in his favor; and we combated for him a while with some hopes of success.

There was much scribbling pro and con upon the occasion; and finding that tho' an elegant preacher he was but a poor writer, I lent him my pen and wrote for him two or three pamphlets, and one piece in the *Pennsylvania Gazette* of April 1735.

The pamphlets were titled: *A Defense Of the Rev. Mr. Hemphill's Observations: or, an Answer to the Vindication of the Reverend Commission,* October 30, 1735; and *Dialogue Between Two Presbyterians,* April 10, 1735.

Pamphlets written by Franklin contained numerous statements of faith, as recorded in *The Christian Pamphlets of Benjamin Franklin* (Fortenberry, 2014); and *Franklin on Faith: The Definitive Guide to the Religion of the First American* (Fortenberry, 2015):

> • "Christ gave himself for us that he might redeem us from all Iniquity, and purify to himself a peculiar people zealous of Good–Works. And there is scarcely a chapter in the whole Gospels

or Epistles from which this Doctrine can't be prov'd."

• "It is the duty of every Christian Minister to explode such errors which have a natural tendency to make men act as if Christ came into the world to patronize vice, and allow men to live as they please."

• "I would advise these Reverend Gentlemen impartially to read the Scriptures."

• "They should acknowledge Jesus Christ to be the Messiah promised by the Prophets, the Son of God."

• "Those Doctrines delivered by our Savior and the Apostles, which are absolutely necessary to be believed, are so very plain, that the meanest capacities, may easily understand 'em."

• "Christ by his Death and Sufferings has purchas'd for us those easy Terms and Conditions of our Acceptance with God, propos'd in the Gospel, to wit, Faith and Repentance."

• "I am conscious I believe in Christ, and exert my best endeavors to understand his Will aright, and strictly to follow it."

In defense of Hemphill, Franklin wrote that:

Christianity ... is plainly nothing else, but a second Revelation of God's

Will founded upon the first Revelation, which God made to us by the Light of Nature.

Despite Franklin's efforts, Rev. Samuel Hemphill was removed from preaching at the church. After this, Franklin ceased attending the church, though he continued to support it financially.

Franklin also printed the works of Presbyterian Rev. Alexander Craighead:

*The 1743 Renewal of the Scottish National Covenant* (1744); and *The Solemn League and Covenant* (1748).

Rev. Craighead had anonymously written the first treatise denouncing the King of England in 1743. He left Pennsylvania for North Carolina to be the pastor of Sugar Creek Presbyterian Church in Mecklenburg County.

There his teaching is thought to have inspired the 1775 Mecklenburg Declaration of Independence, a precursor to Jefferson's 1776 Declaration of Independence.

Franklin published works of other prominent Presbyterian and Great Awakening ministers:

- Ralph Erskine, who wrote in *The Gospel Sonnets*, "Faith, without trouble or fighting, is a suspicious faith; for true faith is a fighting, wrestling faith";

- Josiah Smith, Pastor in Charleston, South Carolina, who supported Rev. Whitefield. He was captured and made a prisoner of war during Revolution;

- Henry Scougal, who wrote *The Life of God in the Soul of Man*, which was praised by Rev. Whitefield;

- Samuel Finley, a trustee and president of Princeton, who influenced Benjamin Rush, a signer of the Declaration of Independence; and Richard Stockton, a signer of the Constitution. Samuel Finley's great-grandson was Samuel Finley Breese Morse, developer of the telegraph;

- Gilbert Tennent, whose most famous sermon was "On the Danger of an Unconverted Ministry," whose father founded the Log College – Princeton;

- Samuel Davies, the fourth president of Princeton, who was a missionary to slaves a strong advocate of religious freedom, and who profoundly influenced Patrick Henry;

- Samuel Jacob Blair, who was educated at the Log College, helped train Samuel Davies. Blair's son was the second chaplain of the U.S. House of Representatives.

# FRANKLIN PUBLISHED
# NEW LIGHT REV. WHITEFIELD

Franklin printed the sermons of Great
Awakening evangelist George Whitefield, and as
joint postmaster general of the colonies, helped
to distribute them throughout the country.

Franklin attended Whitefield's Great
Awakening Revival meetings in front of
Philadelphia's Courthouse steps. There were an
estimated 25,000 in attendance. He described in
his *Autobiography*:

> It was wonderful to see the change
> soon made in the manners of our
> inhabitants.
>
> From being thoughtless or indifferent
> about religion, it seemed as if all the
> world were growing religious, so that
> one could not walk thro' the town in an
> evening without hearing psalms sung in
> different families of every street.

George Whitefield wrote to Franklin in 1752:

> My Dear Doctor ... I find that you
> grow more and more famous in the
> learned world.

Franklin wrote to Whitefield:

> I sometimes wish you and I were
> jointly employed by the Crown to settle

a colony on the Ohio ... a strong body of religious and industrious people! ...

Might it not greatly facilitate the introduction of pure religion among the heathen, if we could, by such a colony, show them a better sample of Christians than they commonly see in our Indian traders?

In 1764, Franklin wrote to Whitefield, ending with the salutation:

Your frequently repeated Wishes and Prayers for my Eternal as well as temporal Happiness are very obliging. I can only thank you for them, and offer you mine in return.

In Whitefield's last surviving letter, he shared his desire that both he and Franklin would:

... be in that happy number of those who is the midst of the tremendous final blaze shall cry Amen. (Revelations 7:12; 19:4).

John Adams described Franklin:

The Catholics thought him almost a Catholic. The Church of England claimed him as one of them. The Presbyterians thought him half a Presbyterian, and the Friends believed him a wet Quaker.

In 1749, Franklin highlighted "public religion" for its "usefulness to the public" in his *Proposals*

*Relating to the Education of Youth in Pennsylvania*:

> History will also afford the frequent opportunities of showing the necessity of a public religion, from its usefulness to the public; the advantage of a religious character among private persons ... and the excellency of the Christian religion above all others, ancient or modern.

Franklin experienced his era's version of the "cancel culture," as he explained in the *Pennsylvania Gazette*, June 10, 1731:

> Being frequently censur'd and condemn'd by different persons for printing things which they say ought not to be printed, I have sometimes thought it might be necessary to make a standing apology for myself, and publish it once a year.

He wrote:

> That when truth and error have fair play, the former is always an overmatch for the latter.

Franklin lived out his views of being involved and doing things.

# FRANKLIN'S DAY OF FASTING

When Spain and France threatened war on the English colonies, Franklin proposed a General

Fast which he published in his *Pennsylvania Gazette*, December 12, 1747.

He wrote in his *Autobiography*:

> Calling in the Aid of Religion, I propos'd to them the Proclaiming a Fast, to promote Reformation, and implore the Blessing of Heaven on our Undertaking. They embrac'd the Motion, but as it was the first Fast ever thought of in the Province, the Secretary had no Precedent from which to draw the Proclamation. My Education in New England, where a Fast is proclaim'd every Year, was here of some Advantage. I drew it in the accustomed Stile, it was translated into German, printed in both Languages and divulg'd thro' the Province."

Franklin called citizens to both prayer and defense in his Proclamation for a General Fast:

> December 9, 1747,
>
> Forasmuch as it is the Duty of Mankind, on all suitable Occasions, to acknowledge their Dependence on the Divine Being to give Thanks for the Mercies received, and no less to deprecate his Judgments, and humbly pray for his Protection:
>
> And as the Calamities of a bloody War, in which our Nation is now engaged, seem every Year more nearly

to approach us ... and there is just Reason to fear, that unless we humble ourselves before the Lord, and amend our Ways, we may be chastised with yet heavier Judgments:

We have therefore thought fit ... to appoint ... a Day of Fasting and Prayer; exhorting all, both Ministers and People ... to join with one Accord in the most humble and fervent Supplications, that Almighty God would mercifully interpose, and still the Rage of War among the Nations, and put a Stop to the Effusion of Christian Blood ... and ... confound the Designs and defeat the Attempts of its Enemies, and unite our Hearts, and strengthen our Hands in every Undertaking that may be for the Public Good, and for our Defense and Security in this Time of Danger.

Franklin did not just organize prayer. He also organized a militia, quite an impressive achievement given the colony was largely Quaker, German Pietist, Mennonite, Brethren, and others who were known for being nonviolent and politically uninvolved. Franklin got around this by having it be a "volunteer" militia – no one was forced to join.

Soon, ten thousand volunteered. It was so well-received that it catapulted Franklin into leadership, beginning his political career.

Franklin continued to be involved. In 1732, he began publishing *Poor Richard's Almanack*, which sold 10,000 copies a year. Franklin retired at age 42, taught himself five languages, invented: the rocking chair; the Franklin stove; bifocal glasses; swim fins; a catheter; an odometer for measuring postal routes; a musical instrument called a glass armonica; a long-arm reaching device to get books off high shelves; and the lightning rod which earned him degrees from Harvard and Yale.

He helped found America's first hospital, first postal system, a fire department, a fire insurance company, a public lending library, and the University of Pennsylvania, one of America's oldest institutions of higher learning.

He studied wind speeds and water currents, their depth, speed, temperature, from the West Indies along the Eastern coast of North America, across the Atlantic to Europe, being the first scientist to map the Gulf Stream.

He was a delegate to the Continental Congress, a signer of the Declaration of Independence, the first U.S. Ambassador to France, a signer of the Treaty of Paris which ended the Revolutionary War, Governor of Pennsylvania, a signer of the U.S. Constitution, President of America's first anti-slavery society and petitioned Congress to ban slavery.

He wrote in *Poor Richard's Almanac*, May 1757:

Work as if you were to live 100 years;
pray as if you were to die tomorrow.

❦

# *NEW LIGHTS*

# WHO WERE
# NEW LIGHT PIETISTS?

Martin Luther's personal beliefs gave him the conviction to stand up to the most powerful person in the world, King Charles V of Spain.

Some German princes wanted to break away from Rome and thought this was their chance. They effectively said, kingdom of mine, I just decided you are all now Lutherans. The people in those kingdoms basically responded, okay, we're Lutheran. What do we believe?

So for the people in those kingdoms, it was not necessarily the same personal conviction that Martin Luther had. It is just a new state doctrine. Soon a revival movement started called Pietism.

Lutheran Pietists taught that being a Christian was more than agreeing with state doctrine, even if it was good doctrine. You must have a personal experience with Jesus, and when you do, your life will change and you will no longer do the worldly things you used to do, like go to bars and brothels and lewd theaters ... and get involved in worldly government.

Wait, what's that last thing?

Yes, government. It is filled full of worldly

people, so if you are really a Christian, you will not be involved.

That was the beginning of this idea that it is more spiritual not to be involved in politics. That we should just preach the Gospel, not get involved in carnal issues. Faith is so personal it is only personal.

People with this attitude are subtly implying, I am more spiritual than you are because I am not involved. You have not reached my higher spiritual level. You are still carnal, at a lower level, because you are concerned about temporal things like government. I just focus on the pure Gospel.

That is where that idea came from — German Pietists. It did not come from the Calvinist Puritans, Pilgrims, or Congregationalists.

In Germany, this turned into the two kingdom concept: the kingdom of the government and the kingdom of the church, and the two do not touch. It was an "either/or" model, individuals were either involved in church affairs or involved state affairs, but not both. This was different from the Puritan covenant model, where individuals were expected to be involved in both church affairs and state affairs.

In Germany, some princes were known to donate money to the Pietists so they would teach their people not to get involved in the prince's business. Today, wealthy globalists are donating money to woke pastors and churches so they will teach not to be involved in politics, so they can work their anti-biblical agenda without resistance.

One need only ask, if all the sincere, holy followers of Jesus withdraw from being involved in politics, who is left to be involved? The less holy? The less holy would tend to yield to their selfish ambitions, becoming power–hungry and oppressive.

Four centuries of that teaching allowed Hitler to seize control of the government and put Jews in the train cars, who cried out for help as they went past churches. Shockingly, the church response was, well, that is the government doing that, and we are the church. We cannot get involved in government business because we are "holy" — so let us just sing praise songs to Jesus louder.

Can anybody see that there is something wrong with this picture?

# ZINZENDORF & THE MORAVIANS

Similar to William Penn's "holy experiment" of Pennsylvania was Zinzendorf's Moravian "Herrnhut" on the eastern border of Germany.

In the year 1700, when William Penn was 60 years old, Count Ludwig von Zinzendorf was born, being a descendant of Maximilian I, the Holy Roman emperor from 1493 to 1519.

Zinzendorf's father died when he was six weeks old, leaving him an estate in the area of Germany called Saxony. He was raised by his Pietist Lutheran grandmother, Henrietta Catharina, Baroness von Gersdorff.

Zinzendorf became friends with Lutheran Pastors Johann Andreas Rothe of Berthelsdorf and Melchior Schäffer of Görlitz. They, together with Friedrich von Watteville, sought to spread "Pietism," a religious revival movement similar to that led by Jan Hus three centuries earlier.

Jan Hus followed the example of England's John Wycliffe, who preached the Scriptures in the common language of the people. Hus was put on trial at the Council of Constance. When asked to recant, he answered: "I would not for a chapel of gold retreat from the truth!"

Hus was burned at the stake on July 6, 1415. In his dying words, he predicted God would raise up others who would bring reformation. Sixty-eight years after Hus' death Martin Luther was born.

Hus made a great impact. For the next two centuries, the majority of Czech people were Hussites, called "Brothers of the Law of Christ" or *Unitas Fratrum* – Unity of Brethren.

Unfortunately for them, they were defeated during the Thirty Years War at the Battle of the White Mountain, November 8, 1620. Followers were hunted down, arrested, killed, or forced by the government to abandon their views.

This was just one of the many European wars which resulted in thousands of religious refugees.

In 1722, at the age of 22, Count Ludwig von Zinzendorf attempted a William Penn-type "holy experiment" in Europe. He opened up his German Berthelsdorf estate in Moravia near the Bohemian Czech Kingdom, to be a place of refuge for the different denominations of persecuted Christians displaced by the Thirty Years War.

Zinzendorf helped them build a village called Herrnhut, meaning "The Lord's watchful care."

Discord almost ended this experiment of Christian unity, but Zinzendorf decided they needed to have a communion prayer service, August 13, 1727. After they forgave each other and reconciled, they experienced a visitation of the Holy Spirit. They prayed all night, then all the next day, the next night and the next day.

They took turns with the responsibilities of cooking meals, caring for the children, and managing the farm, while keeping the prayer meeting going. They prayed all week, all month, all year. That prayer meeting went on uninterrupted twenty-four hours a day, seven days a week for over one hundred years!

Zinzendorf declared "If I have one passion, it is Jesus, Jesus only."

Moravians were a revival movement within Saxony's Lutheran Church. Like the Quakers, Moravians emphasized having a personal relationship with Jesus. Both movements were known for being non-violent and tolerant.

Similar views were held by the Mennonites, followers of the Dutch Anabaptist leader Menno Simons (1496–1561). When Mennonites were persecuted in the German Kingdom of Prussia, they fled. Some immigrated to America and others to Russia where they were called Kulaks.

A Mennonite leader named Jakob Ammann led a movement in 1693 to reform the Mennonite church in Switzerland and South Germany. His followers were called Amish and many of them settled in William Penn's "holy experiment" of Pennsylvania where they stayed uninvolved in government.

Count Ludwig von Zinzendorf and the Moravians had a church structure of forming themselves into *banden*, or small bands of believers — voluntary groups that encouraged spiritual growth and accountability.

They de-emphasized class and wealth distinctions, focused on equality before God, and began the tradition of calling each other "brother" and "sister." Women were given greater freedom to share their faith. The Moravian motto was:

In essentials, unity; in nonessentials, liberty; and in all things, love.

A Great Moravian Revival began among the youth. Young men and women, or young couples would pray and feel led by the Holy Spirit to go to the Caribbean, North and South America, Central America's Mosquito Coast, the Arctic, Africa, and the Far East.

They received no financial support. There were no checks in the mail. Once in a country, Moravians would learn the language and work multiple jobs in order to support themselves and be a Christian witness. Their selfless hard work developed into what was called the "Protestant work ethic."

Imagine all that energy that young people have being used, not to tear things down and set fires, but instead being used to risk their lives going across the world to hostile places to spread the Gospel. Moravians were the first Protestant denomination to minister to slaves.

Some Moravians settled Bethlehem, Pennsylvania, in 1740. In 1741, Count Zinzendorf traveled to America and visited with leaders, including Ben Franklin. He spent seven weeks visiting Indian tribes in forests of Pennsylvania, being the first person of European nobility to meet with Indian chiefs.

Moravians settled Winston–Salem, North Carolina, in 1752. They founded missions among native Americans: Lenape in Pennsylvania, Mohican in New York, and Cherokee in Georgia.

Moravian Pietist teachings produced a political non-involvement called "pacificism." This reputation helped them to enter kingdoms around the world by assuring the king that they were not there to overthrow the government.

Unfortunately, the Pietist pacifist teaching which aided Moravians in gaining entrance into other countries was misapplied in America, where the citizens were the king. It produced a spiritual, yet uninvolved, negligent citizenry.

# THE WESLEYS
# AND THE METHODISTS

In 1736, a group of Moravians were on a ship, the *Simmons*, headed to Georgia. Who else was on the ship? Charles Wesley, who was to be the secretary of James Oglethorpe, and his brother, John Wesley, who was to be the first Anglican minister to the colony.

The ship was caught in a terrible storm on the

sea. The main sail was shredded and water was flooding in. The Wesleys panicked in fear. They ran through the tossing and turning ship only to make it to the area where the Moravians were.

The Wesleys were taken aback when they saw the Moravians singing praise songs to the Lord throughout the storm.

John Wesley later wrote in his *Journal*, January 25, 1736:

> The sea broke over, split the main sail in pieces, covered the ship, and poured in between the decks, as if the great deep had already swallowed us up. A terrible screaming began among the English.
>
> The Germans [Moravians] calmly sang on. I asked one of them afterwards, "Were you not afraid?" He answered, "I thank God, no." I asked, "But were not your women and children afraid?" He replied, mildly, "No; our women and children are not afraid to die."
>
> From them I went to their crying, trembling neighbors, and pointed out to them the difference in the hour of trial, between him that feareth God, and him that feareth him not.
>
> At twelve the wind fell. This was the most glorious day which I have hitherto seen.

The Wesleys realized that the Moravians had a

personal experience with the Lord and an absolute trust in the Lord that they did not have.

The Wesleys were not successful in Georgia and sailed back to England where they met another Moravian missionary, Peter Bohler, who invited them to a prayer meeting.

On May 24, 1738, John Wesley went to a Moravian prayer meeting in London:

> In the evening, I went very unwillingly to a Society in Aldersgate–Street, where one was reading Luther's preface to the Epistle to the Romans …

> About a quarter before nine, while he was describing the change which God works in the heart through faith in Christ, I felt my heart strangely warmed … I felt I did trust in Christ; Christ alone, for salvation; and an assurance was given me, that He had taken away my sins, even mine, and saved me from the law of sin and death.

John Wesley had a personal experience with Jesus. In 1738, he traveled to Germany and lived at Herrnhut with the Moravians for eight months. After seeing them up-close, he described their faith as "the religion of the heart." He met Zinzendorf, communicating in Latin, a language they both knew.

Wesley went back to England and started the Methodist revival movement within the Anglican

Church similar to the Moravian Pietist revival movement inside of the Lutheran Church.

Wesley taught that religion was more than state-mandated doctrine, even if it was good doctrine. You had to have a personal experience with Jesus. The Wesleys introduced this belief to their friend, George Whitefield, who preached up and down the colonies seven times, spreading the Great Awakening Revival.

What did the revival emphasize? A personal experience with Jesus, after which a person's life would change. They would no longer do worldly things, including government. To some, it became so personal that it was *only* personal.

Part of Wesley's "method" that was borrowed from the Moravians was believers meeting in small bands, joining together in homes to pray, study Scriptures and support each other.

∽

## GEORGE WHITEFIELD AND THE GREAT AWAKENING

In 1738, Rev. George Whitefield first arrived in Savannah, Georgia. In the next 32 years before his death, he traveled to America seven times, preaching some 18,000 sermons. Ben Franklin printed Whitefield's sermons and distributed them throughout the colonies.

Franklin helped build an auditorium in Philadelphia for Whitefield to preach in.

Franklin wrote of Rev. Whitefield:

> Multitudes of all denominations attended his sermons ... It was wonderful to see the change soon made in the manners of our inhabitants.

The Great Awakening Revival had a profound effect, as noted by Sarah Pierrepont Edwards, wife of Jonathan Edwards, who wrote to her brother in New Haven regarding effects of the preaching of George Whitefield:

> It is wonderful to see what a spell he casts over an audience by proclaiming the simplest truths of the Bible ...

> Our mechanics shut up their shops, and the day laborers threw down their tools to go and hear him preach, and few return unaffected.

The Revival helped unite them prior to the Revolutionary War.

# MUHLENBERGS

Henry Muhlenberg was the founder of the Lutheran Church in America, He had two sons who were Pietist Lutheran ministers: John Peter Muhlenberg, pastor of Emanuel Lutheran Church in Woodstock, Virginia, and Frederick Augustus Muhlenberg, pastor of Christ Lutheran Church, in New York City.

On March 23, 1775, John Peter Muhlenberg heard Patrick Henry's "Give me liberty or give me death" speech. He was deeply inspired and approached General George Washington and offered to help. Washington appointed him as a colonel and told him to go get his men.

On January 21, 1776, thirty-year-old Pastor John Peter Muhlenberg preached from the Book of Ecclesiastes 3:1 (RSV):

> For everything there is a season, and a time for every matter under heaven ... a time of war, and a time of peace ...
>
> In the language of the Holy Writ, there is a time for all things. There is a time to preach and a time to fight. And now is the time to fight.

At the end of his sermon, he took off his black clerical robe to reveal his officer's uniform in the Continental Army. He had an altar call and 162 men came forward. Outside the church, drums rolled.

Together with 138 men from surrounding churches, the men kissed their wives goodbye and rode off to become the 8th Virginia Regiment.

*Silence Equals Consent*

Muhlenberg fought in the battles of Brandywine, Germantown, Monmouth and Yorktown. He was promoted to major-general. After the Revolutionary War, he was elected to the first session of the U.S. Congress, then elected as a U.S. Senator.

His statue is in the U.S. Capitol, depicted taking off his black robe and displaying his uniform and sword.

During the War, his brother, Frederick Muhlenberg, wrote to John Peter:

> You have become too involved in matters which, as a preacher, you have nothing whatsoever to do.

John Peter wrote back accusing Frederick of being a Tory British sympathizer.

Frederick wrote back he could not serve two masters, based on the German concept of the two kingdoms: the kingdom of the government and the kingdom of the church, and the two do not touch.

Then the British invaded New York, and fire spread through the city. Frederick watched his church burn down. He fled the city with his wife and children.

Then Frederick's attitude changed to: maybe I should get involved. Then he became active in the Revolution.

After the Revolution, Frederick, like his brother John, was elected to Congress. There, he was chosen to be the first Speaker of the U.S. House of Representatives.

Think of it. The first Speaker of the U.S. House of Representatives was Lutheran Pastor Frederick Augustus Muhlenberg, who went from being a non-involved Pietist to getting involved and making a difference.

Of note is that both he and his brother where in that first session of Congress which passed the Bill of Rights, the first Ten Amendments.

There are two signatures on the proposed Bill of Rights sent to the states for ratification, that of Vice President John Adams, in his role as the President of the U.S. Senate; and Frederick Augustus Muhlenberg, the Speaker of the House.

Does anybody honestly think that these two pastors would vote to outlaw themselves? Would they say, pastors are not supposed to be involved in politics, even though we are pastors and we are involved?

No. The First Amendment, as well as the first Ten Amendments, were meant to be limits, or handcuffs, on the new Federal government, hamstringing it from becoming a big centralized monster like that of King George III.

The First Amendment limits Congress, the Federal lawmaking body:

*Silence Equals Consent*

> Congress shall make no law respecting an establishment of religion, or prohibiting the free exercise thereof.

The writers of the U.S. Constitution were preoccupied with how to take the concentrated power of a king and separate it.

They wanted to prevent a return to one-person rule. They intended to prohibit a president from using emergencies to usurp power and rule as a tyrant through mandates and executive orders.

Sir William Blackstone, who was extensively quoted by the Founding Fathers, wrote in his *Commentaries on the Laws of England*:

> It is better that ten guilty persons escape than one innocent suffer.

The Constitution takes a king's power to rule and separates it into three branches, then separates it further between federal and state levels, then ties it up with ten handcuffs – the Bill of Rights.

They wanted to guarantee to individuals their Creator-given rights shall not be infringed on by overbearing government bureaucracy.

This is similar to how God took Nimrod's power at the Tower of Babel and scattered it.

The Constitution is a balancing act of people giving up enough power to create a government yet retaining enough power to control it. The state needs sufficient power to control the people but the people need sufficient power to control the state.

Citizens need to be protected from criminals on the street as well as from criminals in government.

It is understood that some government is needed to protect citizens' rights from a mob of selfish individuals who commit crimes, yet if those selfish individuals find a way to get elected and use their public offices to commit crimes, there needs to be a way to remove them.

Fallen, selfish human nature is the problem, and we all struggle with it since Adam and Eve sinned.

It is like a teeter–totter: if citizens have more internal moral restraints, order can be maintained in a society with fewer external government restraints. The reverse is true: if citizens have fewer internal moral restraints the government will enact more external restraints to maintain order.

John Adams explained October 11, 1798:

> Our Constitution was made only for
> a moral and religious people.

Amid the backdrop of the French Revolution and its Reign of Terror, British statesman Edmund Burke wrote in *A Letter to a Member of the National Assembly*, 1791:

> What is liberty without wisdom and
> without virtue? It is the greatest of all

possible evils; for it is folly, vice, and madness, without restraint.

Men are qualified for civil liberty in exact proportion to their disposition to put moral chains upon their own appetites; in proportion as they are disposed to listen to the counsels of the wise and good in preference to the flattery of knaves ...

Burke continued:

Society cannot exist, unless a controlling power upon will and appetite be placed somewhere; and the less of it there is within, the more there must be without.

It is ordained in the eternal constitution of things, that men of intemperate minds cannot be free. Their passions forge their fetters.

Noah Webster wrote "Political Fanaticism, No. III," published in *The American Minerva*, September 21, 1796:

The reason why severe laws are necessary in France, is, that the people have not been educated republicans – they do not know how to govern themselves (and so) must be governed by severe laws and penalties, and a most rigid administration.

# PURITANS VERSUS PIETISTS

Presbyterians and Puritans advanced the covenant concept in England. Some fled to America, and some remained in England where they fought a Civil War, 1639–1653, and chopped off the head of King Charles I.

Puritans set up a type of "American experiment," a covenant government called the Commonwealth of England. It ended in 1660, with the return of Charles II to the throne, restoring the monarchy.

In America, Pilgrims, Puritans, Baptists, Dutch Reformed, Congregationalists, followed by Presbyterians, Quakers and others, ran both their churches and their colonial governments bottom-up, with citizen–believers being involved in both church and state.

In Germany, the Pietist movement began, emphasizing a personal relationship with Jesus. To some, though, it was so personal, it was *only* personal. They advocated separating from everything worldly, including government. A major Pietist group were the Moravians, who sent out missionaries around the world, sparking revivals.

The Pietists had a reputation for political non-involvement. This helped them gain access into kingdoms around the world as kings did not feel threatened by them.

The Pietists influenced John and Charles Wesley, who influenced George Whitefield, who preached the Great Awakening Revival in America. It was a powerful revival, emphasizing a personal relationship with Jesus, but a byproduct was it was so personal it was only personal, resulting in many withdrawing from being involved in government.

So where Pietist non-involvement teachings helped them gain entrance into kingdoms around the world, in the American Colonies, which had self-governing representative governments, Pietism produced negligent and irresponsible citizens.

# OLD LIGHT–NEW LIGHT CONTROVERSY

As the decades passed, the covenant plan became somewhat formal, rigid, and strict. As good as the plan was, the teaching of it became spiritually dry. Faith, to some, was so planned that it was *only* a plan. Some interpreted the doctrine of God's foreknowledge of who would believe as an excuse to neglect preaching the Gospel.

Puritans became nicknamed "Old Lights."

In the 1700s, evangelical "New Lights" came on the scene. They spread the Great Awakening Revival through the colonies, teaching that religion was more than a plan. One had to have a personal experience with Jesus.

Where did the New Lights come from?

In 1517, Martin Luther started the Reformation because he had a personal experience after reading "the just shall live by faith." It was so personal to him that he was willing to stand trial before the Holy Roman Emperor and reportedly proclaimed: unless you can prove me wrong from Scripture, here I stand so help me God.

They effectively said: kingdom of mine, I just decided you are all now Lutherans. The people's response was essentially, okay, but what do we believe?

So for people in their kingdoms, it was not necessarily the same personal experience that Martin Luther had. It is just a new state doctrine.

In response, a revival movement started called Pietism. Pietists taught that being a Christian was more than a plan or agreeing with state doctrine, even it if was more Scripture-focused, you had to have a personal experience with Jesus, and when you did, your life would change, and you would withdraw from worldly things, including politics. This was the beginning of the teaching that it is more spiritual to "just preach the Gospel" and not to participate in politics; that it is holier to withdraw from the public square. This is similar to gnosticism, where to be spiritual one had to completely be separate from the temporal, material world. Gnostics taught that the spiritual world is good, and the material world bad.

This, though, conveniently sidesteps the verses Matthew 6:10, "Thy will be done *on Earth* as it is in Heaven"; and Genesis 1:28, "Be fruitful, and multiply, and replenish *the Earth*, and subdue it." One translation says "govern it."

To Pietists, faith became so personal that it was *only* personal. Some exhibited a "holier-than-thou" virtue-signaling attitude, condescendingly implying that they had reached a higher spiritual level by abandoning civic responsibility and not caring what kind of country they left their children.

The Pietist attitude is reminiscent of Eli, when told by the Prophet Samuel that the Lord would judge his house for ever because he allowed his sons to sin, Eli said, "It is the Lord, let Him do what seemeth Him good" (I Samuel 3:18); or when the Prophet Isaiah told Hezekiah that his sons would be eunuchs in the palace of Babylon, Hezekiah said "Is it not good, if peace and truth be in my days." (II Kings 20:19).

Contrast that to how David responded when the Prophet Nathan told him that because of David's murder of Uriah and adultery with Bathsheba that his son would die, "David therefore besought God for the child; and fasted, and went in, and lay all night upon the earth" (II Samuel 12:16); or when the Prophet Gad told David that because he sinned by taking a census, the Lord would judge the Israelites, David interceded to the Lord, "Lo, I have sinned, and have done wickedly: but these sheep, what have they done?" (II Samuel 24: 17).

Proverbs 13:22:

> A good man leaves an inheritance to his children's children.

Non-involvement came from 18th century German Pietists. It did *NOT* come from 17th century Puritans. The Puritan covenant required that everyone participate in both church and state.

In Germany, the Pietist's view turned into the two kingdom concept: the kingdom of the government and the kingdom of the church, and the two do not touch. It was an "either/or" model, individuals were either involved in church affairs or involved state affairs, not both.

Pietists taught that being holy required Christians be like Eli and Hezekiah, and surrender society to an anti-Christian fate of judgment. This withdrawal attitude spread to other denominations, replacing the Puritan participation attitude.

As the *more* spiritual people withdrew from politics, the *less* spiritual people were left in

*Silence Equals Consent*

politics. Being less spiritual, they yielded to selfish ambition, became power–hungry politicians, not content with controlling government, but also being tempted to control the church.

Pietists created a self-fulfilling prophecy – withdraw from government because it is so ungodly, and guest what, it becomes so ungodly.

President Harry Truman stated April 3, 1951:

> Without a firm moral foundation, freedom degenerates quickly into selfishness and ... anarchy. Then there will be freedom only for the rapacious and ... more unscrupulous than the rank and file of the people.

When those filled with the Word of God and the Spirit of God withdraw, society falls into immoral chaos, which is followed by people panicking and surrendering their freedoms to usurping politicians who promise to "fix" the lawlessness created by the pastors who taught Christians to not be involved.

Like the childhood game King-of-the-Hill, ambitious politicians concentrate power to push their agenda. It will be a shock to those pastors who taught people not to be involved when they get persecuted by those usurping politicians that their negligence helped elect.

Jesus said in Mark 9:50 "Salt is good: but if the salt have lost his saltness, wherewith will ye season it? Have salt in yourselves." Salt is a preservative, without it, meat rots.

∽

# PARTICIPATION
# VERSUS WITHDRAWAL

The defining word for Puritans was "participation." Individuals were expected to be involved in both church affairs and state affairs. The defining word for Pietists was "withdrawal." Individuals were expected to withdraw from worldly things, including government.

In Germany, some princes even donated money to the Pietists so they would teach their people not to get involved in the prince's business. Today, wealthy globalists are donating money to woke seminaries so they will teach pastors not to be involved in politics, allowing them to carry out their anti-biblical agenda without interference.

Four centuries of Pietist teaching allowed Hitler to seize power and put Jews on train cars to be transported to their deaths. As they went passed churches, they cried out for help. The churches' response was, that was the government doing that and the church is not suppose to be involved in government business because of the two kingdom teaching, so church members should just sing praise songs to Jesus louder.

Can anybody see that there is something wrong with this picture?

Why can't it be both? Christians should have a personal relationship with God and also be involved in government, so they can preserve a nation where their children can have a chance to have a personal relationship with God. Because if we do not get involved, the unholy agenda that is being pushed on the youth in school, in music, and in entertainment, will undermine their children's belief in God.

The most important thing is to bring people to Christ; but the second most important thing is to preserve the freedom to do the most important thing.

*Silence Equals Consent*

∾

# SILENCE EQUALS CONSENT

# IS IT HOLY TO BE SILENT?

There is an important question that needs to be addressed: is it holy to be silent and uninvolved? Should we withdraw and wait for Jesus to return?

To those who think it is "holier" not to be involved, what do you do with Numbers 30. It is the silence equals consent chapter. There are a half dozen scenarios, such as:

> If a daughter binds herself with a vow while living in her father's house in her youth, and her father hears her vow ... and holds his peace, then all her vows shall stand.
>
> But if her father overrules her on the day that he hears, then none of her vows ... shall stand; and the Lord will release her.

That has come down to us as vows in a wedding ceremony, and the pastor tells the church members, if you are silent when you hear these vows you are giving your consent; "speak now, or forever hold your peace."

*The Book of Common Prayer*, 1549, stated:

> If anyone present knows of any reason that this couple should not be joined in holy matrimony, speak now

or forever hold your peace.

It is called the Rule of Tacit Admission. *Black's Law Dictionary* gives the definition:

> An admission reasonably inferable from ... a party's failure to act or speak.

In Latin, the phrase is:

> *Qui tacet consentire videtur, ubi loqui debuit ac potuit* (He who is silent is taken to agree, when ought to have spoken and was able to.)

Plato wrote in *Cratylus,* (c.360 B.C., 435b):

> I shall assume that your silence gives consent.

In trial law it is called Tacit Criminal Admission:

> The doctrine of tacit admissions is firmly entrenched in state and federal criminal prosecutions. Courts have assumed that a reasonable juror could find a person more likely to deny an accusation he knows to be false than one he knows to be true.

David Matson of Experienced Criminal Defense Lawyers Nationwide, wrote "Supreme Court Rules Silence Can Be Evidence of Guilt":

> The Supreme Court ruled that a suspect's silence during pre-arrest questioning can be considered evidence of guilt ...
>
> The case in question involved

Genovevo Salinas, convicted of shooting two brothers in 1992. During informal questioning and before his arrest, officers engaged Salinas, who answered most of their questions willingly. But, when they asked Salinas if the shotgun shells found at the murder scene would match his weapon, he fell silent. This, the prosecutor said at trial, was evidence of his guilt.

In his appeals, attorneys for Salinas argued that his silence was protected by the Constitution. The Supreme Court felt otherwise. In their opinion, the Supreme Court justices said Salinas was not protected because he did not "expressly invoke the privilege against self-incrimination."

It is in trademark law. If you design a trademark and someone copies and is using it, if you are silent and do nothing to defend it, you can lose your exclusive right to it. David H. Schwartz published December 7, 2023, "Defend Your Trademark Or You Could Lose It":

Take Swift Action Against Infringements: If you find your trademark being infringed upon, act swiftly. This might involve issuing cease and desist letters or taking legal action. Remember, inaction can weaken your trademark rights.

In real estate law, if a squatter lives on your

property and you are silent, not attempting to charge them rent or evict them, you can lose your ownership of the property through "adverse possession." State Property Management, LLC, published "Squatting Laws in Florida":

> Squatters ... can legally claim ownership of your property through an adverse possession claim ... (usually abandoned, foreclosed, or otherwise unoccupied building) after living in it for a continuous period of time. In the state of Florida, for an adverse possession claim to be valid, a squatter must have lived in the property for at least 7 years ...

> To get rid of squatters in Florida, you need to file an unlawful detainer lawsuit ... You must first notify the squatter with an eviction notice.

In financial or tax situations, if creditors or tax collectors wait too many years before trying to collect on a debt, they may have exceeded the statute of limitations and forfeited claims to repayment. Consumer Financial Protection Bureau published April 14, 2023, "Can debt collectors collect a debt that's several years old?":

> In many states, statutes of limitations are in place to prevent creditors and debt collectors from using legal action to collect on an older debt ... Most states or jurisdictions have statutes of

> limitations between three and six years
> ... A lawsuit filed after the statute of
> limitations expires is a violation of the
> Fair Debt Collection Practices Act,

With certain civil and criminal cases, if the injured person is silent and waits several years before bringing legal action, they may have exceeded the statute of limitations and missed their chance for justice. Investopedia published "Statute of Limitations: Definition, Types, and Example" by Christina Majaski, January 4, 2024:

> A statute of limitations is a law that
> defines the maximum amount of time in
> which parties involved in a dispute must
> initiate legal proceedings following an
> alleged offense.

The Rule of Tacit Admission is even in the U.S. Constitution, Article I, Section VII:

> Every Bill which shall have passed
> ... shall ... be presented to the President
> ... If any Bill shall not be returned by
> the President within ten days ... after it
> shall have been presented to him, the
> same shall be a Law, in like manner as
> if he had signed it.

The President's silence is legally interpreted as his consent "in like manner as if he had signed it." His silence equals his signature.

If the silence of church members gives consent to wedding vows, then their silence gives consent to other things.

If babies are being killed in a community and church members know about it and are silent, then they are giving their consent to killing babies.

Moreover, if you give consent to sin, you share in the guilt as an accessory — and you will share in the judgment. An accessory includes someone who had knowledge of a crime and did not attempt to prevent it, or after-the-fact, when they learned who committed it, did not make it known.

Leviticus 20:1–5 (NIV):

> Any Israelite or any foreigner residing in Israel who sacrifices any of his children to Molech is to be put to death …
>
> If the members of the community close their eyes when that man sacrifices one of his children to Molech … I Myself will set My face against him and his family and will cut them off from their people together.

*Coffman's Commentaries on the Bible* stated of Leviticus 20:4–5:

> The imputation of guilt to those who concealed crime is taught here, a principle which has found its way into the laws of all nations.

*Henry's Complete Commentary on the Bible:*

> That all his aiders and abetters should be cut off likewise by the righteous hand

of God. If his neighbors concealed him, and would not come in as witnesses against him,–if the magistrates connived at him, and would not pass sentence upon him, rather pitying his folly than hating his impiety,–God himself would reckon with them.

"Connive" is defined in *The Merriam–Webster Dictionary* as:

> To pretend ignorance of or fail to take action against something one ought to oppose.

*Gill's Exposition of the Entire Bible* stated of Leviticus 20:4–5:

> And if the people of the land do any ways hide their eyes from the man ... though they know what he is about to do, or has done, yet they shut their eyes willfully, or look another way; or, however, wink and connive at his wickedness, and will not discover him, and bear witness against him; or if a court of judicature, before whom he comes, does not take the evidence of his crime, nor condemn for it, or are negligent in punishing him as the law directs, a gift having blinded their eyes, or they careless and remiss in their duty: when he giveth his seed unto Molech; a crime so heinous and abominable: and ... do not bring witness against him ... Then I will set my face against ... that

man that sees him do the act, and winks at it, or the judge that connives at him, and will not condemn him ... and will cut him off.

Chuck Smith, founder of Calvary Chapel of Costa Mesa, gave insight into Leviticus 20 in *Smith's Bible Commentary (2014)*:

> Chapter twenty, now God begins to get a little heavier ... I don't know what's gone wrong with our judicial system, but we are far more interested in protecting the rights of the criminals than we are of the innocent victims ...

> We are living in a crazy, corrupt world that's gone wild. It's because we've forsaken the law of God ...

> If a father sacrificed his child to Molech, he was to be put to death ... And if you in any wise hide your eyes from him who has sacrificed his children to Molech, and you don't kill him, then God will set his face against you, and against your family, to cut you off.

*LifeNews.com* reported the headline "California Bill Would Allow Killing Babies in Infanticide Up to 28 Days After Birth." Thankfully, enough pastors and church members could not be silent and pressured politicians in Sacramento to reword the legislation.

The Apostle Paul did not throw a stone or say a word, yet he knew by his silence he shared in the guilt of Stephen's death. Acts 22:20:

> And when the blood of thy martyr Stephen was shed ... I also was standing by consenting to his death.

Proverbs 24:11–12 (TLB) warns:

> Rescue those who are unjustly sentenced to death; do not stand back and let them die. Do not try to disclaim responsibility by saying you did not know about it. For God, who knows all hearts, knows yours, and he knows you knew! And He will repay everyone according to his deeds.

You cannot see a need and "hide thyself." Deuteronomy 22:1–4:

> Thou shalt not see thy brother's ox or his sheep go astray, and hide thyself from them: thou shalt in any case bring them again unto thy brother ...

> In like manner shalt thou do ... with all lost things of thy brother's ... thou mayest not hide thyself.

> Thou shalt not see thy brother's ass or his ox fall down by the way, and hide thyself from them: thou shalt surely help him to lift them up again.

During the Great Depression, October 18,

1931, President Herbert Hoover led a drive to mobilize church organizations to provide relief:

> This great complex, which we call American life, is builded and can alone survive upon the translation into individual action of that fundamental philosophy announced by the Savior nineteen centuries ago ... Modern society cannot survive with the defense of Cain, 'Am I my brother's keeper?'"

In the Book of Esther 4:14 (NAB), Mordecai tells Esther of the government mandate to kill Jews:

> If you now remain silent, relief and deliverance will come to the Jews from another source; but you and your father's house will perish. Who knows — perhaps it was for a time like this that you became queen?

# THE SIN OF OMISSION

Aaron's silence kept him out of Promised Land. Numbers 20 recorded:

> Moses and Aaron went ... unto the door of the tabernacle ... And the Lord spake unto Moses ... take the rod ... gather the assembly ... thou and Aaron

> ... Speak to the rock ... and it shall give forth water ...
>
> And Moses lifted up his hand, and with his rod he smote the rock twice ... and the water came out abundantly ...
>
> And the Lord spake unto Moses ... Aaron will not enter the land ... because both of you rebelled against my command at the waters of Meribah.

"Both of you rebelled"? "Aaron will not enter the land"! Why? Aaron did not hit the rock. He did not even say a word!

Yes! That is just it. There were only two people at the door of the tabernacle: Moses and Aaron. Aaron heard God tell Moses "speak to the rock."

When Moses lifted up the rod the first time and in anger hit the rock, it probably took Aaron by surprise. That was Moses' sin.

When Moses lifted up the rod the second time, Aaron knew what was coming and he did not protest. He did not say, Moses, stop! I heard God say speak to the rock!

No, Aaron was silent, and in that instant he was guilty. Moses' was a sin of commission; Aaron's was a sin of omission.

Leviticus 5:1 (EHV) states:

> A person sins because he did not speak up, even though he was an eyewitness to a case or knew what

happened ... anyone who failed to testify, he is guilty.

Another example of this is in the Book of Jeremiah 36:21–25:

> King Jehoiakim sent ... to fetch Jeremiah's scroll ... and Jehudi read it in the ears of the king and ... all the princes ...
>
> Now the king sat in the winter palace ... and there was a fire on the hearth burning before him ... Whenever Jehudi had read three or four columns of Jeremiah's scroll, the king cut them off with a scribe's knife and threw them into the fire ...
>
> Yet the princes showed no fear, nor did they tear their clothes ... nor any of his servants ... though Elnathan, Delaiah and Gemariah urged the king not to burn the scroll.

It is clear that the princes, by not protesting, were guilty of giving their consent to the burning of Jeremiah's scroll.

Martin Luther King, Jr., stated:

> He who passively accepts evil is as much involved in it as he who helps to perpetuate it ... He who accepts evil without protesting it, is really cooperating with it ... In the end, we will remember not the words of our enemies but the silence of our friends.

❦

# GERMAN CHURCH WAS SILENT?

During WWII, Germany's two kingdom concept caused the "kingdom of the church" to remain silent as the "kingdom of the government" – the National Socialist Workers' Party was killing Jews. Some could stay silent no longer, such as Dietrich Bonhoeffer, who helped start the Confessing Church movement.

A truth associated with Bonhoeffer's courageous stand is: "Silence in the face of evil is itself evil: God will not hold us guiltless."

Pro-Life speaker Seth Gruber wrote:

> Led by Hans Scholl and his sister Sophie, the White Rose Resistance was a small collective of Christian students who secretly wrote and distributed leaflets all around Germany, criticizing the Nazis and inspiring others to resist them.

> On February 18th, 1943, Hans and Sophie walked the halls at the University of Munich, placing hundreds of their leaflets in the open. The janitor caught them in the act and Sophie and her brother were sentenced to death by guillotine.

> On the eve of her beheading, Sophie spoke some of her final words: "Such

a fine, sunny day and I have to go. But what does my death matter, if through us, thousands of people are awakened and stirred to action?" As the blade prepared to fall, Sophie said, "The sun still shines!"

While we face a silent and far more deadly holocaust, your sacrifice will water the seeds of resistance. Thousands will be awakened and stirred to action.

And the White Rose will blossom.

Sophie Scholl stated: "We are Christian and we are German. Therefore, we are responsible for Germany."

## COURAGE TO SPEAK UP

Many preachers have delivered outstanding sermons, but in times of moral confusion, it would be better to hear a pastor who is not as eloquent but has courage to speak the truth than to hear the most articulate sermon by a coward.

Deuteronomy 20:1–4:

When thou goest out to battle against thine enemies, and seest horses, and chariots, and a people more than thou, be not afraid of them: for the Lord thy God is with thee, which brought thee up out of the land of Egypt ...

> Let not your hearts faint, fear not, and do not tremble, neither be ye terrified because of them; For the Lord your God is he that goeth with you, to fight for you against your enemies, to save you.

Dutch Reformed Pastor Abraham Kuyper, who was prime minister of the Netherlands, 1901–1905, wrote:

> The calling of the Christian absolutely does not lie in the sphere of the church alone ... Christians also have a calling in the midst of the life of the world. And the question as to how this is possible, how it is conceivable that a child of God should still be involved with a sinful world, has a brief, clear, and simple answer: it can and must be because God himself is still involved with that world.

Albert Einstein addressed the Chicago Decalogue Society, February 20, 1954:

> In long intervals I have expressed an opinion on public issues whenever they appeared to me so bad and unfortunate that silence would have made me feel guilty of complicity.

Poet Robert Frost is attributed with the line:

> A liberal is someone who won't take his own side in a fight.

James 4:17 (NKJV) states:

*Silence Equals Consent*

> To him who knows to do good and does not do it, to him it is sin.

John the Baptist warned in Matthew 3:8–10 (NIV):

> Bear fruits worthy of repentance ... Every tree which does not bear good fruit is cut down and thrown into the fire.

Jesus warned in Matthew 7:16–23:

> Ye shall know them by their fruits ... Every good tree bringeth forth good fruit ... Every tree that bringeth not forth good fruit is hewn down, and cast into the fire. Wherefore by their fruits ye shall know them. Not every one that saith unto me, Lord, Lord, shall enter into the kingdom of heaven; but he that doeth the will of my Father.

What if someone takes God's name in vain? Exodus 20:7 and Deuteronomy 5:11 state:

> The LORD will not hold him guiltless that taketh his name in vain.

What if you are silent when someone takes God's name in vain? Proverbs 29:24 explains that if you hear someone swearing and taking God's name in vain and do not "bewrayeth it":

> Whoso is partner with a thief hateth his own soul: he heareth cursing, and bewrayeth it not.

General Washington would not put up with cursing and swearing. He ordered July 4, 1775:

> The General … requires … observance of those articles of war … which forbid profane cursing, swearing and drunkenness; And … requires … punctual attendance of Divine Services.

It was not that long ago that parents did not put up with children taking God's name in vain. In the popular movie, *Indiana Jones and The Last Crusade,* there is a scene where Indiana, played by Harrison Ford, is riding a motorcycle, with his father, played by Sean Connery, in the attached passenger carriage. Indiana takes God's name in vain, and his father reaches up and slaps him. The music plays a serious note as Sean Connery points his finger in the face of Indiana and says "That's for blasphemy!"

Leviticus 5:1 (LEB):

> A person sins in that he hears the utterance of a curse (swearing) and he is a witness … if he does not make it known, then he shall bear his guilt.

# ELI DID NOT RESTRAIN SONS

When Eli was High Priest, he did not commit sin, but his sons did and he did not restrain them when they "lay with the women that assembled at the door of the tabernacle of the congregation."

*Silence Equals Consent*

I Samuel 3:11 (NIV) recorded:

> Then the LORD said to Samuel … "I will carry out against Eli everything I have spoken … because his sons blasphemed God and he did not restrain them."

The Prophet Samuel did not sin, but his sons did, and because he failed to correct them it resulted in the entire nation sinning.

I Samuel 8:

> And it came to pass, when Samuel was old, that he made his sons judges over Israel … And his sons walked not in his ways, but turned aside after lucre, and took bribes, and perverted judgment.

> Then all the elders of Israel gathered themselves together, and came to Samuel unto Ramah, And said unto him … "Thy sons walk not in thy ways: now make us a king to judge us like all the nations" …

> The Lord said unto Samuel … "They have not rejected thee, but they have rejected Me, that I should not reign over them" …

> I Samuel 12:19:And all the people said unto Samuel, "Pray for thy servants unto the Lord thy God that we die not, for we have added unto our sins this evil to ask a king."

David's eldest son, Amnon, sinned by raping his half-sister, Tamar, yet David was silent and did not reprimand him.

2 Samuel 13:21 (NRSV) recorded:

> When King David heard of all these things, he became very angry, but he would not punish his son Amnon, because he loved him, for he was his firstborn.

As a result of his silence, David's son, Absalom, Tamar's brother, killed Amnon then led a rebellion against David almost costing him the throne.

Leviticus 19:17 (CEV) teaches:

> It is wrong not to correct someone who needs correcting.

# DO BOTH: LOVE AND REBUKE

Everyone knows Leviticus 19:18 (NIV):

> Love your neighbor as yourself.

Do you know the verse right before it? Leviticus 19:17:

> Confront your neighbor directly so you will not be held guilty for their sin.

The same verse in the Holman Standard Bible translation is:

> Rebuke your neighbor directly, and you will not incur guilt because of him.

The Israelites were loving each other and correcting each other. There were no police in the ancient Hebrew Republic. Everyone was taught the Law and everyone helped enforce the Law.

Proverbs 9:8 states:

> Rebuke a wise man and he will love thee.

Ecclesiastes 7:5 states:

> It is better to hear the rebuke of the wise than ... the song of fools.

Proverbs 28:23 states:

> He that rebuketh a man afterwards shall find more favor than he that flattereth with the tongue.

Revelation 3:19 states:

> As many as I love, I rebuke and chasten.

Hebrews 12:5 states:

> My son, despise not the chastening of the Lord, nor faint when thou art rebuked of him.

Titus 2:14–15 states:

> These things speak, and exhort, and rebuke with all authority.

I Timothy 5:20 states:

> Them that sin rebuke before all.

II Timothy 4:2 states:

> Preach the word, be instant in season, out of season, reprove, rebuke.

Titus 1:11–13 states:

> There are many unruly and vain talkers ... who subvert whole houses ... Wherefore rebuke them sharply.

Titus 2:14–15 states:

> These things speak, and exhort, and rebuke with all authority.

Nehemiah 5: states:

> Then I consulted with myself, and rebuked the nobles and the rulers.

II Peter 2:16 states:

> But [Balaam] was rebuked for his iniquity: the dumb ass speaking with man's voice forbad the madness of the prophet.

Luke 17:3:

> If your brother sin ... rebuke him.

Luke 9:55 states:

> But Jesus turned, and rebuked them, and said, Ye know not what manner of spirit ye are of.

Luke 23:40 states:

> But the other thief answering rebuked him, saying, Dost not thou fear God, seeing thou art in the same condemnation.

It can be done politely in love, as mentioned in I Timothy 5:1:

*Silence Equals Consent*

Rebuke not an elder, but entreat him as
a father and the younger men as brethren.

"Entreat" means petition respectfully. It does
not mean remain silent. It should be done in love.
Ephesians 4:15: "But speaking the truth in love."

∽

# BE LIKE JESUS

Being like Jesus does not mean being silent. It may be a new thought to some, but Jesus did not pet lambs all day long. He spoke the truth even if it made people uncomfortable.

From birth it was clear that Jesus would meet resistance. Mary and Joseph were told by Simeon:

Behold, this Child is destined for the fall
and rising of many in Israel, and for a sign
which will be spoken against (Luke 2:35).

His first sermon ended with them wanting to push him off a cliff (Luke 4:29). Another sermon ended and hearers "took they up stones to cast at him" (John 8:59); and again "Then the Jews took up stones again to stone him" (John 10:31).

After multiplying loaves and fishes, Jesus had a crowd following Him for a free lunch. He gave a sermon in John 6:24–68, appearing to intentionally shake away those following Him for wrong, materialistic reasons.

> Jesus answered them ... "Most assuredly, I say to you, you seek Me, not because you saw the signs, but because you ate of the loaves and were filled" ...
>
> Then they said to Him, "Lord, give us this bread always." And Jesus said to them, "I am the bread of life ... The Jews then complained about Him, because He said, "I am the bread which came down from heaven" ...
>
> Therefore many of His disciples, when they heard this, said, "This is a hard saying; who can understand it?" ... From that time many of His disciples went back and walked with Him no more.

Jesus did not run after them and try to get them to come back. Instead:

> Then Jesus said to the twelve, "Do you also want to go away?" But Simon Peter answered Him, "Lord, to whom shall we go? You have the words of eternal life."

When a Pharisee noticed Jesus did not wash His hands, Jesus rebuked him (Luke 11:37–54):

> Ye Pharisees make clean the outside of the cup and the platter; but your inward part is full of ravening and wickedness. Ye fools, did not he that made that which is without, make that which is within also? ...
>
> Woe unto you, Pharisees! For ye love the uppermost seats in the synagogues, and greetings in the markets ... Hypocrites! for ye

are as graves which appear not, and the men that walk over them are not aware of them ...

Then answered one of the lawyers ... Master, thus saying thou reproachest us also. And he said, Woe unto you also, ye lawyers! for ye laden men with burdens grievous to be borne, and ye yourselves touch not the burdens with one of your fingers ...

Woe unto you, lawyers! for ye have taken away the key of knowledge: ye entered not in yourselves, and them that were entering in, ye hindered ...

And as he said these things unto them, the scribes and the Pharisees began to urge him vehemently, and to provoke him to speak of many things: Laying wait for him, and seeking to catch something out of his mouth, that they might accuse him."

Matthew 16:13–16 states:

Jesus ... asked His disciples ... "Who do men say that I, the Son of Man, am?" So they said, "Some say John the Baptist, some Elijah, and others Jeremiah or one of the prophets."

He said to them, "But who do you say that I am?" Simon Peter answered and said, "You are the Christ, the Son of the living God."

Most readers skip past it, but who did people mistake Jesus for? John the Baptist, Elijah, and

Jeremiah. What did John the Baptist do? He stood up to the corrupt King Herod. What did Elijah do? He stood up to corrupt King Ahab. What did Jeremiah do? He stood up to corrupt King Zedekiah.

∽

# WATCHMAN

Believers are called to be watchmen, as the Lord told Ezekiel, 3:17–21:

> Son of man, I have made thee a watchman unto the house of Israel ...

> When a righteous man doth turn from his righteousness, and commit iniquity ... he shall die: because thou hast not given him warning ... his blood will I require at thine hand.

> Nevertheless if thou warn the righteous man, that the righteous sin not, and he doth not sin, he shall surely live, because he is warned; also thou hast delivered thy soul.

What if you get a hateful response when you warn people? Jesus replied in John 15:18 (NLT):

> If the world hates you, you know that it hated Me before it hated you ... If they persecuted Me, they will also persecute you.

Matthew 10:22 (NKJV):

> And you will be hated by all for My name's sake. But he who endures to the end will be saved.

Luke 6:22-23:

> Blessed are ye, when men shall hate you, and when they shall separate you from their company, and shall reproach you, and cast out your name as evil, for the Son of man's sake. Rejoice ye in that day, and leap for joy: for, behold, your reward is great in heaven.

Peter's preaching produced a similar response: some said, what must we do to be saved, and others sought to arrest him and put him in jail

Paul's preaching also had a similar response: some searched the Scriptures and believed, and others sought to stone him.

If Jesus is inside of us, we cannot but expect that people respond to us similarly to how they responded to Jesus. Perhaps if we don't get a similar response, maybe we should check if we are bringing Jesus with us!

When Jesus came into a place, His presence was a catalyst which caused a reaction. Some humbly accepted His message and by faith were healed and saved; others pridefully rejected His message, hardened their hearts and plotted to kill Him. The place was not the same when He left.

To the humble, Jesus was as loving as can be, but to the prideful He was tough.

James 4:6 (NKJV) and I Peter 5:5 (NKJV) explained:

> God resists the proud, but gives grace to the humble.

In Psalm 18:24–26, David wrote:

> With the merciful thou wilt shew thyself merciful ... and with the froward thou wilt shew thyself froward.

II Samuel 22:27:

> With the pure thou wilt shew thyself pure; and with the froward thou wilt shew thyself unsavoury.

If you approach God humbly, and confess that you are a sinner, you will find grace; if you approach God pridefully, you will find judgment.

Matthew 21:44 (AMP):

> And he who falls on this Stone will be broken ... but he on whom it falls will be crushed.

Like magnets with one side that repels and the other side that attracts. Psalm 51:17:

> The sacrifices of God are a broken spirit; a broken and a contrite heart, O God, thou wilt not despise.

If you cowardly tone back proclaiming the truth of the Gospel for fear of getting a negative response, you will have toned it back so much you will also not get a positive response.

Revelation 21:8 (NKJV):

> But the cowardly [fearful] ... shall have their part in the lake which burns with fire.

❧

# OBEY GOD RATHER THAN MEN

Some people revealed their pride by wanting to be "liked" by others so much they would not confess Christ publicly. John 12:42–43 recorded:

> Even among the rulers, many believed in Him, but because of the Pharisees they did not confess Him, lest they should be put out of the synagogue; for they loved the praise of men more than the praise of God.

Jesus stated in John 5:44:

> How can you believe, who receive honor from one another, and do not seek the honor that comes from the only God?

Peter was with a group around a fire and a girl got in his face and said, you were with Jesus. You can just picture Peter looking around the fire with everyone staring at him. Realizing he was about to be kicked out of this group of strangers he cowardly responded: "Woman, I know him not." Fear of what people think of you is a real fear. I Samuel 15:24: "Saul said unto Samuel, I have sinned ... because I feared the people, and obeyed their voice." Jeremiah 38:19 recorded that when King Zedekiah was told God would spare Jerusalem if he surrendered to the Chaldeans, he refused: "I am afraid of the Jews that are fallen to the Chaldeans, lest they deliver me into their hand, and they mock me."

After the resurrection, though, Peter was filled with the Holy Spirit and he no longer cared about what men thought of him. He only cared about what God thought. The High Priest said in Acts 5:27-29:

> "Did we not strictly command you not to teach in this name? And look, you have filled Jerusalem with your doctrine, and intend to bring this Man's blood on us!" But Peter and the other apostles answered and said: "We ought to obey God rather than men."

Maybe one of the evidences of being filled with the Holy Spirit is having the courage not to be silent, so speak up, to confront corrupt government, not caring if you are kicked out of a group or what people will say about you.

God told Jeremiah (1:8):

> Be not afraid of their faces; for I am with thee to deliver thee!

We are to make decisions based on God's Word, not make decisions based on what other people will think about us. Exodus 23:2 warns::

Thou shalt not follow a multitude to do evil; neither shalt thou speak in a cause to decline after many to wrest judgment:

The Complete Jewish Bible gives the translation:

Do not follow the crowd when it does what is wrong; and don't allow the popular view to sway you into offering testimony for any cause if the effect will be to pervert justice.

The same verse in the Easy-To-Read version is:

Don't do something just because everyone else is doing it. If you see a group of people doing wrong, don't join them. You must not let them persuade you to do wrong things—you must do what is right and fair.

*Silence Equals Consent*

❧

# *JESUS LOVES THE LITTLE CHILDREN*

# GOSPEL OF ANTICHRIST?

Are we headed back in the direction of the government dictating beliefs by punishing people who believe differently, like Nebuchadnezzar who attempted to kill Shadrach, Meshech and Abednigo; or the Sanhedrin which arrested Peter; or Henry VIII who executed William Tyndale; or Charles II whose Star Chamber sentenced dissenters to branded and imprisoned?

*The Telegraph*, April 1, 2024, headlined "Diversity training 'forces workers to hide beliefs' for fear of losing job":

> Free Speech Union found that 31 percent had left a former employer because of their endorsement of 'woke' ideology.

Some believers are content with being "holy" and withdrawing, enjoying their personal faith, but by doing so, they are allowing government to undermine their children's faith.

These believers sit quiet while schools teach lies, such as: there is no God, or if He exists, He is messed up, making mistakes, putting men in women's bodies, and condemning them to lifetimes of expensive operations and pharmaceuticals. Schools present God as confused, powerless, or worse yet, sadistic.

Moreover, schools teach children to experiment sexually, showing them explicit library books. This is contrary to the Bible, which teaches sex is sacred and to be experienced only in the confines of a marriage between a man and a woman.

If sex outside of marriage is not sin, then arguably there are no sins. If there are no sins, you certainly do not need a Savior who "will save His people from their sins" (Matthew 1:21).

Amazing! Adults who believe the Gospel are allowing children to be taught an antichrist gospel!

If church members know that schools in their communities are teaching sexual views different from what Jesus taught, and those church members are silent — they are giving their consent!

The lines are being drawn.

On Easter Sunday, the holiest day of the year for Christians, President Biden proclaimed Trans Visibility Day, 2024. Many considered this a direct attack on Christianity. Mainstream media recoiled at the response from the Trump campaign:

> It is appalling and insulting that Joe Biden's White House prohibited children from submitting religious egg designs for their Easter Art Event, and formally proclaimed Easter Sunday as "Trans Day of Visibility" ...

> We call ... [for] an apology to the millions of Catholics and Christians across America who believe tomorrow is for one celebration only — the resurrection of Jesus Christ!

Aggressive promotion of this sexual agenda is creating an intentional division – a socialist tactic to destabilize a nation so that government can seize more power.

This is similar to ancient Israel's sexual immorality during the period of the Judges, when "every man did that which was right in their own eyes." In the chaos, people surrendered their freedom to a king.

Those who are promoting abortion of unborn infants are also promoting trans surgeries on children. It is as if the same spirit that mutilates children inside the womb wants to mutilate them outside the womb.

Groups that advocate mutilating children are virtue–signaling that they "care" for children. The question is: do they really?

They engage in psychological projection, accusing "non-affirming" parents of pushing children to depression and suicide, when research is showing the opposite, that trans teaching and trans surgeries are responsible for that.

*Silence Equals Consent*

# RESCUE THE INNOCENT

A church song that many grew up with is, "Jesus loves the little children, all the children of the world." It is the most basic of all God-given instincts to defend innocent children.

How then could Christians adults be lulled into not caring what happens to children? Never in human history have there been headlines like:

*TheGatewayPundit.com* published February 20, 2024: "Male Student Who Identifies as Transgender Injures Three Girls During Basketball Game—Causing Opposing Team to Forfeit."

*MSN.com* published November 5, 2023: "Male Field Hockey Player on Female High School Team Knocks Out Girl's Teeth Mid-Game, Causing 'Significant' Facial Injuries."

*Breitbart.com,* March 27, 2024: "Parents Outraged After Women's Soccer Team with Five Trans Players Wins Tournament"

*WesternJournal.com,* February 5, 2024: "Five Transgendered Players Dominate a Single College Volleyball Game While Females Are Relegated to the Bench."

*TheGatewayPundit.com,* March 27, 2024: "Trans Man Wins Women's Weightlifting Title – Apparently They Don't Have to Play Pretend Anymore."

*Outkick.com*, March 24, 2024: "Two Female

Darts Players Quit Dutch Team After Male Wins Men's And Women's Pro Events In Same Week."

Joe Rogan, March 7, 2024, interviewed competitive swimmer Riley Gaines, who champions preserving women's sports from biological male competitors.

Many Christians are silent while teachers use "social–emotional" learning techniques which weaponize peer pressure to manipulate a child's desire to be accepted by shaming them into embracing unbiblical behavior.

They teach the "pyramid of oppression," with "cisgendered" (people who believe humans are male and female) on the top as the bad oppressors, who oppress everybody else down the pyramid.

Since no child wants to be a bad oppressor, they identify with anything else down the pyramid: intersexual, bisexual, transsexual, asexual, LGBT, anything, but just not the cisgendered, because they are taught they are "bad."

It is working! *AllSides.com* published October 11, 2022: "Maryland's largest school district sees 500 percent increase of non-binary, trans students."

*The Washington Stand* published October 13, 2022: "Trans–Identifying Students Increase 991% Over Two Years in Wealthy DC Suburb."

Children are exposed to explicit library books

and drag queen story hours, yet some Christians would rather be silent and give their tacit approval.

The church tolerating this behavior is one of the signs of the last days. Jesus rebuked the church at Thyatira for allowing sexual sin (Revelation 2:18-20):

> These things saith the Son of God, who hath his eyes like unto a flame of fire ... I have a few things against thee, because thou sufferest that woman Jezebel, which calleth herself a prophetess, to teach and to seduce my servants to commit fornication.

Jesus rebuked the church at Pergamos for allowing sexual sin (Revelation 2:14):

> I have a few things against thee, because thou hast there, them that hold the doctrine of Balaam, who taught Balac to cast a stumblingblock before the children of Israel, to eat things sacrificed unto idols, and to commit fornication.

# GENDER CONFUSION

For all of recorded human history, there have been men and women, boys and girls. When did this gender confusion agenda begin?

In the 1960s, a New Zealand psychologist named John Money coined the terms "sexual orientation" and "gender role." He believed a child's identity was malleable between infancy and two years old.

In 1966, infant twin boys, David and Brian Reimer, were brought to him. David had a permanent injury from an improper circumcision. Money attempted to turn David into a girl.

After years of traumatic surgeries and psychological therapy sessions, David committed suicide and Brian died of an overdose. John Money's experiment was condemned internationally, yet his theories persisted.

In an open letter, July 3, 2023, in *The Wall Street Journal,* 21 medical researchers wrote:

> [The] claim that gender transition reduces suicides is contradicted by every systemic review.

*New American* published "New Study Debunks 'Trans' Theory: "Transitioning" Kids Does NOT Save Lives" by Selwyn Duke, February 24, 2024:

> "Would you rather have a living son or dead daughter?" This question, often asked marketing–style of parents whose child desires so-called gender reassignment procedures, is not just unethical, says the leader of a groundbreaking new study on sexually confused youths.

"It is also," says psychiatrist Dr. Riittakerttu Kaltiala, "not based on facts" ... Administering ... "gender–reassignment" treatments does not lower sexually confused youths' suicide rate ...

Making these findings even more compelling is that Dr. Kaltiala actually helped pioneer ... "transgender medicine" in Finland ... Research teams have evaluated the available studies ... They've all concluded that the "science" was not scientific at all ...

The findings are that neither going to a gender clinic nor undergoing gender–transition treatment was tied to an independent significant difference in the suicide rate ... Treatment didn't improve their mental health ...

Dr. Paul McHugh, former chief of psychiatry at Johns Hopkins Hospital ... explained ... "It proves not easy nor wise to live in a counterfeit sexual garb. The most thorough follow-up of sex-reassigned people — extending over thirty years and conducted in Sweden, where the culture is strongly supportive of the transgendered — documents their lifelong mental unrest.

Ten to fifteen years after surgical reassignment, the suicide rate of those who had undergone sex-reassignment surgery rose to 20 times that of comparable peers" ...

"At Johns Hopkins, after pioneering sex change surgery, we demonstrated that the practice brought no important benefits. As a result, we stopped offering that form of treatment."

✍

# LONELIER

*The Daily Signal* headlined "Biden's Department of Re-Education," March 8, 2024: "Studies show so-called gender–affirming care leaves people feeling lonelier and more suicide–prone."

*Human Events* reported September 21, 2023:

> 34% of children on puberty blockers from UK gender clinics suffered mental health issues, new findings show.

*The Daily Caller* published the article by Ailan Evanson, July 14, 2023: "Doctors Around The World Condemn Top Medical Organization For Pushing Youth Sex Changes 'Without Evidence.'"

*The Washington Stand* headlined "Gender Affirming' Surgery Leaves People Lonelier and Depressed, Study by Transgender Surgery Department Chairman Finds," June 2, 2023:

The University Medical Center Hamburg-Eppendorf, May 30, 2022 ... found that transgender surgeries do not improve mental health [but] make people feel lonelier ...

Mary Beth Waddell, director of federal affairs for family and religious liberty at the Family Research Council, told *The Washington Stand.*

"One study showed that the suicide completion rate for those that had undergone surgery was 19 times higher than the general population" ...

Evidence shows the best thing parents can do for children questioning their biological identity is to prevent them from having permanently disfiguring surgeries or potentially sterilizing hormone injections.

"Even the American Psychiatric Association, which supports gender identity ideology, acknowledges that a high percentage of children will desist from feelings of dysphoria if allowed to go through puberty naturally" ... Waddell said.

# PUSHBACK

*ThePostMillennial.com*, February 10, 2024:

Planned Parenthood recommends toddlers be asked if they are 'a boy or a girl' by parents – Whatever answer the toddler gives, parents should accept it and treat them as such, according to the guidance.

Candi Cushman of The Family Foundation wrote on February 6, 2024: "Trans Indoctrination for Six Years Old – Parents Speak Out."

*The New York Post* published February 1, 2024: "Family flees US after teacher spurs, hides 10-year-old daughter's gender 'transition.'"

*New York Post,* January 29, 2024, "Montana Family Loses Their 14 Year-old After Opposing Gender Transition."

*DailyMail.com* reported atrocities:

Pink-haired Portland surgeon who performs sex-change surgery on trans CHILDREN admits they face lifetime of infertility, incontinence and sexual dissatisfaction, in now deleted video – Horrified viewers likened the "evil" procedures to Nazi-era experiments.

It now appears transgender surgeries do not turn a boy into a girl, they turn him into a eunuch.

*FaithWire.com*, February 14, 2024, Billy Hallowell wrote: "'Gender Nightmare' – Why Even Secular People Are Sounding the Alarm on 'Medical Atrocities,' Changing the Trans Debate":

Brandon Showalter's documentary–style podcast ... features interviews with detransitioners, parents whose kids have become entrapped in the gender nightmare ... "There are families, and children, and young people who have had their lives completely destroyed by this," he said. "These are medical atrocities."

*DailyWire.com,* February 7, 2024, Matt Walsh wrote:

Government Accidentally Confirms It Has No Real Evidence To Support So-Called 'Gender Affirming Care' For Minors – In response to a Freedom of Information Act Request, HHS produced a grand total of just one document.

*Breitbart.com* reported March 12, 2024: "NHS England Bans Puberty Blockers for Transgender Children, Activists Denounce":

The National Health Service (NHS) in England has issued a ban on puberty blockers for children who identify as transgender ... there not being enough evidence on the procedure's safety or clinical effectiveness.

The U.K. government also endorsed the "landmark decision," hailing it as being in the "best interests of children."

*ChristianPost* reported: "Presbyterian Church of America petitions Biden, protesting trans surgeries for minors: 'Attempting the impossible.'"

❧

# MORE HARM THAN GOOD

*T*he *Connecticut Centinal* published Dr. Joseph Bentivegna's article, "Transgender Medicine – The Monetization of Misery," March 10, 2024:

> Most physicians like myself can make a comfortable living caring for the sick. But if you really want to make big bucks, the way to do so is to convince healthy people that there is something wrong with them ...

> The latest market is to convince people that they were born the wrong gender. This of course is silly. If you have XY chromosomes you are a male and if you have XX chromosomes, you are a female. This applies not only to humans but to the entire mammalian kingdom.

> But some members of my profession are coining money by convincing confused children and adolescents – many with other psychiatric issues – that they are males instead of females or females instead of males.

> They are using hormone treatments to chemically castrate them and, in some instances, subjecting them to brutal

surgical treatments that remove or add breasts and destroy and rearrange parts of their genitalia. This sometimes results in infertility and sexual dysfunction for the rest of their lives ...

Those promoting gender affirming care have characterized their opposition as ... transphobes. They are now encountering a much more formidable group – the trial lawyers ... Doctors have been sued by disgruntled patients who are now infertile and cannot function sexually ...

Gender affirming care has been practiced in Europe ... and the long-term data on its efficacy is now available. And the verdict is that it does more harm than good.

This means that trial lawyers now have convincing expert witnesses to speak to juries.

Dr. Kaltiala ... after a decade of treating this condition and analyzing her data on its efficacy ... wrote "Gender–Affirming Care Is Dangerous. I Know Because I Helped Pioneer It" ... "I felt an increasing obligation ... to speak ... against the widespread transitioning of gender–distressed minors ...

Viewing similar data, England has prohibited gender affirming treatments before the age of eighteen.

# NO LONGER SILENT

*Breibart.com* published "Transgender 'Treatments' for Children One of the 'Greatest Ethical Scandals in Medical History,' French Report States," March 24, 2024.

*The National Review* published the article "'Gender–Affirming Care' is Increasingly Being Recognized as Unscientific."

Ben Shapiro aired an interview, March 27, 2024, "Bad Therapy is Harming Your Kids," with attorney and journalist Abigail Shrier, author of *Irreversible Damage: The Transgender Craze Seducing Our Daughters*, 2020.

On March 14, 2024, Dr. Jordan Peterson retweeted a *London Times* article @jordanpeterson:

> Gender medicine looked like the future. Now, the *Times of London*, one of the most respected newspapers in the world calls it "Quack Medicine" and is urging that it be "reined in entirely."
>
> US media, medical associations, and politicians should follow the UK's lead.
>
> "Quack Medicine: The NHS is right to ban the routine prescription of puberty blockers. Young lives have been damaged by this potentially life–changing treatment

for gender dysphoria."

Dr. Jordan Peterson interviewed detransitioner Chloe Cole, January 3, 2023:

> Jordan: "Consent has to be documented but it also has to be informed and informed means you have to understand what you're consenting to.

> Chloe: "The problem with me starting it so young was not only that I couldn't consent, I couldn't really fathom the full picture of things, you know. I'll never be able to breastfeed. I'll never have that erogenous sensation in my chest back. I do hate to speak about it, but I'm experiencing sexual dysfunction at the age of 18. That's something that women usually go through when they're in their 40s to 50s. How was I supposed to know?"

*TheGateWayPundit.com* reported (9/12/23):

> In an X post ... Chloe Cole said, "Facebook has notified me that my Instagram bio is too 'violent' .... If you think reading it is violent, imagine actually living through all that."

> Cole underwent a double mastectomy of her healthy breasts at age 15, claiming she was rushed into that and other extreme transgender procedures by doctors and therapists given over to

trans ideology, whom she now describes as "butchers and liars."

"It has ruined my life and I will never be the same. I will never get those years that I was supposed to be growing and thriving back," she said ...

Transgender "medicine" has pushed thousands of children like her across the Western world into undergoing cross–sex "surgeries" and hormone "therapies" that do permanent damage to their bodies.

This has led to a worldwide blowback with several European nations banning trans procedures on youth.

PragerU shared a video, "Chloe Cole: Transition Surgery Was the Biggest Mistake of My Life":

During the post-operation process, Chloe began to regret her decision and had to come to terms with the irreversible damage done to her as a minor. She began speaking out against the very people who once celebrated her—and was met with vitriol and hate.

Heartbreaking stories make their way past online censorship of youth admitting trans-surgeries did not bring them the emotional peace they were promised.

A distraught girl posted a video, crying: "I rejected being a woman before I knew what a woman was and now I can never be one."

Another girl posted a video: "I just had my head shaved ... They say I have male pattern baldness and my hair will never come back ... I don't know what to say ... other than ... this is what happens when a girl takes testosterone for five years ... bye."

All the while, one wonders, why has the church been so silent?

❧

# DETRANSITIONERS NOT SILENT

*The New York Times* published the article by Pamela Paul, "As Kids, They Thought They Were Trans. They No Longer Do," February 2, 2024:

> Grace Powell was 12 or 13 ... The narrative she had heard ... was that if you don't transition, you'll kill yourself. At 17, desperate to begin hormone therapy ... She had a double mastectomy the summer before college ... At no point during her medical or surgical transition, Powell says, did anyone ask her about the reasons behind her gender dysphoria or her depression ...

> Powell, now 23 and detransitioned, told me. "But I was told there is one cure and one thing to do if this is your problem, and this will help you" ...

A report commissioned by the National Health Service about Britain's Tavistock gender clinic, which, until it was ordered to be shut down ... noted that

"Primary and secondary care staff have told us that they feel under pressure to adopt an unquestioning affirmative approach and that this is at odds with the standard process of clinical assessment"...

Parents of kids who consider themselves trans say their children were introduced to transgender influencers on YouTube or TikTok ... (or) the classroom, as early as elementary school, often in child–friendly ways through curriculum supplied by trans rights organizations, with concepts like the gender unicorn or the Genderbread person ...

Parents are routinely warned that to pursue any path outside of agreeing with a child's self-declared gender identity is to put a gender dysphoric youth at risk for suicide, which feels to many people like emotional blackmail ...

In May 2017, Kasey Emerick began searching "gender" online and encountered trans advocacy websites ... "I'm thinking, 'Oh my God, I'm having my breasts removed. I'm 17. I'm too young for this,'" she recalled. But she went ahead with the operation. "Transition felt like a way to control something when I couldn't control anything in my life," Emerick explained.

But after living as a trans man for five years, Emerick realized her mental health symptoms were only getting worse. In the fall of 2022, she came out as a detransitioner on Twitter and was immediately attacked ... "I realized that I had lived a lie for over five years" ...

To the trans activist dictum that children know their gender best, it is important to add something all parents know from experience: Children change their minds all the time.

One mother told ... that after her teenager ... pulled back from a trans identity before any irreversible medical procedures – he explained, "I was just rebelling. I look at it like a subculture, like being goth."

# LEGAL ADVOCATES NOT SILENT

Mat Staver of the Liberty Counsel legal advocacy organization, wrote "This Junk Science is Being Exposed," March 11, 2024:

A scientific review of more than 5,000 "gender dysphoria" studies shows that these studies aren't based on science at all, but rather on the political bias of the "gender affirmation" industry and its quest to capture more dollars ...

"Junk science" is being pushed to create a multibillion-dollar industry, and ... ban Christian counseling. Liberty Counsel ... overturned 23 Christian counseling bans ...

We have been told that gender dysphoria must be treated by affirming the patient's delusion and poisoning the patient with cross–sex hormones while waiting for body mutilation surgeries to remove healthy organs. How many times have we been told that "the science is settled"? Well, it turns out "the science" isn't settled ...

Scientists reviewed the compendium of current "studies" on gender dysphoria ... nearly all of the published research around gender affirmation includes significant flaws.

These flaws would never be justified in actual scientific diagnostic procedures without the highly coordinated social and political pressure campaign that the rabid LGBTQ community is waging ...

There is hope. The tide of public opinion is turning. The ugly face of the LGBTQ agenda targeting our children is being revealed and rejected.

Bill Donohue, of the Catholic League advocacy organization, wrote March 11, 2024:

March 12 is Detransition Awareness Day ... Those who are responsible for transgenderism, the pernicious ideology that holds that the sexes are not binary and are interchangeable, will never call attention to this day ...

The tide is turning. The insane idea that biology doesn't matter — we can self-identify our sex — has peaked ...

The Biden administration ... behavioral sciences and the medical community continue to misinform the public. But the good news is that, even there, many are rethinking their position, coming over to our side. Our side is the side of science. Their side is the side of politics.

Jamie Reed ... took a job in 2018 at a transgender center at St. Louis Children's Hospital and saw how children with gender dysphoria are treated. She left last November because of what she witnessed.

"By the time I departed," she wrote, "I was certain that the way the American medical system is treating these patients is the opposite of the promise we make to 'do no harm.' Instead, we are permanently harming the vulnerable patients in our care."

The American College of Pediatricians recently did a review of more than 60 studies on the issue of adolescents who have transitioned.

They concluded that ...there is "no

long-term evidence that mental health concerns are decreased or alleviated after 'gender–affirming therapy'" ...

Therefore ... they "cannot condone the social affirmation, medical intervention, or surgical mutilation of children and adolescents identifying as transgender"...

The Danish Medical Association found their initial well-meaning intentions were based on insufficient evidence—they encouraged transitioning—but came to realize that they were doing more harm than good and sharply reversed course.

Dr. Kaltiala ... knows why so many professionals have been snookered. "Medicine, unfortunately, is not immune to dangerous groupthink that results in patient harm" ... Transgenderism is a monumental fraud.

# LEGISLATORS NOT SILENT

Jack Davis of *WesternJournal.com* wrote "Ohio Legislature Defies Woke Governor, Overrides Veto of Bill Banning Transition Care for Minors," January 24, 2024:

Ohio Senate ... took a buzzsaw to the buzzword of "gender–affirming care." The

Senate voted 23-9 to override Republican Gov. Mike DeWine's veto ... Ohio's state House overrode the veto 65–28 ...

The law allows state licensing boards to penalize health care providers who provide puberty blockers and hormone therapy to minors ...

Students who believe that a transgender athlete has deprived them of an athletic opportunity can sue the school, school district or other organization that might regulate a sport.

"Despite what the liberals say, gender is not assigned at birth, but rather from the moment of conception, you are either male or you are female," Republican Sen. Kristina Roegner said, according to the *Cincinnati Enquirer*.

"There is no such thing as gender–affirming care. You can't affirm something that doesn't exist," she said.

Roegner said all the words in the world will not change biology.

"There are men and there are women and there are boys and there are girls and they are different," she said, according to the *Ohio Capital Journal*.

"Gender is not fluid. There is no such thing as a gender spectrum," she claimed.

As noted by NBC, Roegner said that treating someone for gender dysphoria, the conflict between a person's gender and what they might think they are, "creates, as you can imagine, a permanent patient."

"This is quite a profit center for those hospitals pushing these procedures to teenagers, children. They're not capable of making life–altering decisions," she said.

❦

# AGAINST TRAFFICKING

Jim Caviezel starred in the film *Sound of Freedom*, which drew attention to the silence Americans have towards child sex trafficking. A line in the movie is that drugs can be sold once but a child can be sold ten times a day.

*TheGatewayPundit.com* published February 23, 2023: "Two Colorado Representatives Speak Out After Democrats Unanimously Vote to 'Indefinitely Postpone' Bill Mandating Sentencing Minimums for Child Sex Buyers."

*TheLibertyDaily* shared a Rumble video: "Tim Tebow Chokes Back Tears While Reading 7 Yr Old's Poem About Her Sexual Abuse to Congress," March 6, 2024:

> A young girl who went through extreme abuse for seven years and almost every night she got raped ... and in the middle of her abuse, this is

what she writes ... "can someone please rescue me." This girl, and thousands of boys and girls just like her, they are calling out to you and to me.

*TruthNigeria.com* posted March 12, 2024: "Over 200 School Children Kidnapped in Nigeria in Broad Daylight with No Military or Police Intervention – Is the U.S. Complicit in Slave Trade?":

> "Students were at the assembly ground, reciting the national anthem ... Terrorists ... came on motorbikes" ... Fulani Islamic terrorists ... went methodically for 4 hours to break into residences ...

> Law professor Robert Destro, a former Assistant Secretary of State ... "The U.S. Government has known for years that kidnapping for ransom is a major problem in Nigeria ...

> When the U.S. supports that government with billions in assistance without demanding that at least part of it be used to train and equip local police, we are complicit in that slave trade ...

> Nigeria is the only country in the world where people can get kidnapped by the hundreds with no resistance.

On *Real America's Voice*, July 24, 2023, Natalie Winters, co-host of Steve Bannon's War Room, exposed how Biden's DOJ is hiding child sex trafficking info from Americans:

The Department of Justice erased content from its webpage on child sex trafficking that highlighted the plight of "international sex trafficking of minors" ... The stunning revision comes amidst scrutiny of President Joe Biden's continued incitement of mass migration via America's porous southern border – a prime avenue for child sex trafficking.

Seth Gruber of the Pro-Life "White Rose Resistance," stated in a video "Proof: Abortion is the Root of Leftism – "If Killing Children Is Healthcare, Then Selling Them Is Capitalism."

God hates the heart-wrenching crime of kidnapping so much that in the Old Testament the kidnapper is to be put to death.

This includes whether the kidnapper is caught in possession of their victims or have already sold them. Exodus 21:16 states:

And he that stealeth a man, and selleth him, or if he be found in his hand, he shall surely be put to death.

Deuteronomy 24:7 (NIV) states:

If someone is caught kidnapping a fellow Israelite and treating or selling them as a slave, the kidnapper must die. You must purge the evil from among you.

Where is the outcry from Christians?

❧

# *WHAT WOULD JESUS DO?*

# A MILLSTONE

$A$ scriptural case can be made that God cares about the children. Proverbs 13:22 states:

> A good man leaves an inheritance to his children's children.

God cares about what children are taught.

Genesis 18:19 (AMP) states:

> For I know him [Abraham], that he will teach his children … (to) keep the way of the LORD, to do justice and judgment.

Deuteronomy 4:9; 6:7 (NCV):

> Teach them to your children and grandchildren.

Today the battle is over who gets to teach the children, these precious little girls and boys made in God's image.

A socialist tactic is to guilt-trip Christians into being more Christian than Christ. They say that if you are really Christian you will be silent and tolerate schools teaching your kids a sexual agenda that Jesus would never teach. So if you are really Christian you will not act like Christ!

Would Jesus teach children the trans agenda? We know what Jesus taught. He said in Matthew 19:4:

He who made them at the beginning
made them male and female.

Think of the absurdity – school counselors who cannot even define what a "woman" is think they are capable of telling a little boy he is supposed to be a girl.

Matthew 18:2–10; Mark 9:42 (NIV):

> Jesus invited a little child to stand among them … [and] said ... If anyone causes one of these little ones who believe in Me to stumble, it would be better for him to have a large millstone hung around his neck and to be drowned in the depths of the sea.

> Woe to the world for the causes of sin. These stumbling blocks must come, but woe to the man through whom they come.

It will be a rude awakening for church members who think they are being "holy" and "spiritual" by not being involved when they realize that by their silence they are giving consent to sin — they are inviting the judgment of God upon their heads!

# LOCAL, LOCAL, LOCAL

What is the answer? LOCAL, LOCAL, LOCAL. If we zoom out and look at what is happening in the world, it becomes clear that as more power concentrates into fewer hands globally, God's counterbalance is to get more people involved locally.

There are more church members in a community than vote in school board races. If churches can say, even though we do not agree with every church on everything, none of us are happy with what is going, let's just agree to support some "mama bear" or a concerned father, get them on the school board. Did you know you do not have to have a child in the public school to be on the school board?

Additionally, do not just vote them in, but also support them by showing up early at school board meetings. This would be a first step in carrying out Proverbs 22:6: "Train up a child in the way he should go."

If pastors and church members can just care about what children are being taught in their local schools, things can start to turn around, and all the higher political races will take care of themselves!

Individuals who feel called to run for higher office will have learned how it works. They just want the pastor's approval that it is OK for them to get involved.

# SACRIFICE FOR POSTERITY

America's founders wrote in the Constitution their purpose was to "secure the blessings of liberty to ourselves and our posterity" and in the Declaration, "we ... pledge our lives, our fortunes..."

They were willing to sacrifice their *prosperity* for their *posterity*, yet today many are sacrificing their posterity for prosperity, burdening their children with a bankrupt country in unpayable debt.

George Washington cared about the future generations of children, the "unborn millions."

After he had the Declaration read to his army in July of 1776, his ranks dwindled in just six months from 20,000 down to 2,000, and these had only volunteered for a six-month enlistment, ending in just days. His army had been chased out of New York, across New Jersey, and was now in Pennsylvania. His code word for crossing the Delaware River on Christmas Day evening, 1776, was "Victory or Death."

He wrote in his General Orders, July 2, 1776:

> The time is now near at hand which must probably determine whether Americans are to be freemen or slaves; whether they are to have any property they can call their own ... whether their houses and farms are to be pillaged and

destroyed, and themselves consigned to a state of wretchedness from which no human efforts will deliver them …

The fate of unborn millions will now depend, under God, on the courage and conduct of this army. Our cruel and unrelenting enemy leaves us no choice but a brave resistance, or the most abject submission. We have, therefore to resolve to conquer or die."

Washington had Thomas Paine's *American Crisis* read to his troops:

THESE are the times that try men's souls. The summer soldier and the sunshine patriot will, in this crisis, shrink from the service of their country; but he that stands by it now, deserves the love and thanks of man and woman.

Tyranny, like hell, is not easily conquered; yet we have this consolation with us, that the harder the conflict, the more glorious the triumph. What we obtain too cheap, we esteem too lightly … Heaven knows how to put a price upon its goods; and it would be strange indeed if so celestial an article as freedom should not be highly rated …

God Almighty will not give up a people to military destruction … who have so earnestly … sought to avoid the calamities of war …

Neither have I so much of the infidel in me, as to suppose that He has relinquished the government of the world ... to the care of devils ...

I am as confident as I am that God governs the world, that America will never be happy till she gets clear of foreign dominion ...

Let it be told to the future world, that in the depth of winter, when nothing but hope and virtue could survive, that ... the country, alarmed at one common danger, came forth to ... to repulse it ...

Throw not the burden of the day upon Providence, but "show your faith by your works,' that God may bless you."

It matters not where you live, or what rank of life you hold, the evil ... will reach you ... The blood of his children will curse his cowardice, who shrinks back at a time when a little might have saved the whole ...

I love the man that can smile in trouble, that can gather strength from distress, and grow brave by reflection.

'Tis the business of little minds to shrink; but he whose heart is firm, and whose conscience approves his conduct, will pursue his principles unto death ...

Paine continued:

Not all the treasures of the world ...

could have induced me to support an offensive war, for I think it murder; but if a thief breaks into my house, burns and destroys my property, and ... threatens to kill me, or those that are in it, and to "bind me in all cases whatsoever" to his absolute will, am I to suffer it? ...

Let them call me rebel ... I feel no concern from it ... but I should suffer the misery of devils, were I to make a whore of my soul by swearing allegiance to one whose character is that of a sottish, stupid, stubborn, worthless, brutish man.

I conceive likewise a horrid idea in receiving mercy from a being, who at the last day shall be shrieking to the rocks and mountains to cover him, and fleeing with terror from the orphan, the widow, and the slain of America.

Connecticut Governor Jonathan Trumbull in a letter to General Washington, August of 1776:

In this day of calamity, to trust altogether to the justice of our cause, without our utmost exertion, would be tempting Providence ...

March on! – This shall be your warrant: Play the man for God, and for the cities of our God. May the Lord of Hosts, the God of the Armies of Israel, be your Captain, your Leader, your Conductor, and Saviour. – 2nd Samuel 10:12.

*Silence Equals Consent*

The fate of the world hangs in the balance, and God will call you to "give an account of your stewardship."

∞

# WAITING FOR JESUS TO RETURN

Knowing the mistreatment of innocent children is going on, some church members still remain silent, just waiting for Jesus to come back and rescue them out of this mess.

Some say, the world has to get more evil before Jesus comes back, so just do nothing — even remarking how exciting it is, as the more evil the world gets just means He is coming back sooner.

Question: Who do you think you are going to meet when you are raptured? Jesus! Do you think He loves the children? Yes! Do you think He might wonder why you were silent and did nothing to protect them?

You are not living in Communist China, or North Korea, or Iran, where people have no say in government. All people in those countries can do is suffer and pray.

God has you living in America, a republic, where the citizens are the king and politicians are the servants. You are in charge!

Moreover, even if we can't turn things around in our country, shouldn't we at least try?

∼

# EXPOSING THE CONDITION OF OUR HEARTS

Maybe another way of looking at what is going on is that God is letting the evil be exposed to expose the condition of your heart. To see how much you will put up with?

Like a doctor giving a patient a "stress test," maybe the Lord is watching to see what it will take to get us to do something.

*USA TODAY,* December 12, 2023, "'Disgusting' Satanic Temple display at state capitol in Iowa sparks free speech battle."

*KAIY Christian Magazine,* February 12, 2024 "University of Houston Will Display Satanic Pro-Abortion Statue for all of 2024."

*NATIONAL REVIEW,* May 22, 2023, "Target Partners with Satanist Brand to Create Items for "PRIDE" Collection."

*AFA,* September 2, 2022, "Disney and FXX Air New Demonic Series 'Little Demon'" featuring the teenage daughter of Satan, portraying Satan as good for wanting to give humans enlightenment and God as evil for keeping humanity suppressed?

*WORLD,* February 10, 2023, "Satanism on display at Grammy Awards – Musical artists don't have to believe in Satan to do his bidding."

*GatewayPundit.com,* February 5, 2024, "Another Satanic Display at Grammy Awards: Singer Performs Satanic Ritual with Demon Sucking Blood and Blood Leaking from Walls."

*WAVE,* December 14, 2023, "Satanic Temple plans 'After School Satan Club' at another elementary school" "Sparks Controversy."

*The Guardian,* December 14, 2023, "Uproar as after–school Satan club forms at Tennessee elementary school."

*ActionNews 5,* January 10, 2024, "Launch of 'After School Satan Club' draws protest at Chimneyrock Elementary."

*The Los Angeles Times*, January 24, 2024, "After School Satan Club is coming to Orange County."

Will you, by your silence, give consent to this? What will it take to get you to speak out? Is your conscience so deadened that those things do not bother you? If you can remain silent in the face of Satanic evil, what does that say about the condition of your heart? Is there no compassion left in you to protect innocent children?

Jesus warned in Matthew 24:12, that in the last days "because evil shall abound, the love of many shall wax cold.'

It is almost as if God is letting the evil be exposed to elicit a response, to see who will be silent, siding with evil, and who cannot be silent anymore. He is putting us in the position of having to choose sides. He is letting evil be exposed to expose the condition of our hearts:

> That the thoughts of many hearts
> may be revealed. (Luke 2:25).

Like the concluding scene in the Wizard of Oz, where the curtain is pulled back to reveal who is behind it, God is pulling back the curtain letting us see Satan behind the world's evil. Will you, by your silence, side with Satan? Or will you take God's side and speak out against evil?

> Jesus spoke in Matthew 25:1–13 (NKJV) of the condition of people's hearts when he returns:The kingdom of heaven be likened unto ten virgins, which took their lamps, and went forth to meet the bridegroom. And five of them were wise, and five were foolish. They that were foolish took their lamps, and took no oil with them: But the wise took oil in their vessels with their lamps. While the bridegroom tarried, they all slumbered and slept. And at midnight there was a cry made, "Behold, the bridegroom cometh; go ye out to meet him."Then all those virgins arose, and trimmed their lamps. And the

*Silence Equals Consent*

foolish said unto the wise, "Give us of your oil; for our lamps are gone out." But the wise answered, saying, "Not so; lest there be not enough for us and you: but go ye rather to them that sell, and buy for yourselves." And while they went to buy, the bridegroom came; and they that were ready went in with him to the marriage: and the door was shut. Afterward came also the other virgins, saying, "Lord, Lord, open to us." But he answered and said, "Verily I say unto you, I know you not." Watch therefore, for ye know neither the day nor the hour wherein the Son of man cometh.

# GOD PUSHING US TO A DECISION

When a cell divides, some of it goes to one side and some to the other. There is nothing left over.

Likewise, some people do evil; and some are silent in the face of evil, and by their silence they are siding with evil.

Then on the other side, there are those of us who say, –I was silent for a long time and tolerated things I did not feel good about. Then I stretched the rubber band and was silent about something else I did not feel good about. Now, though, I am sorry, I cannot go along with a hysterectomy done on an 8-year-old girl just because she went through a tomboy phase. I cannot go along with castrating little boys into eunuchs because they played with their sister's dolls.

You cut the rubber band and it snaps back. A division is made!

Now, since they no longer care what people think about them, they are bolder for Jesus than ever before!

⊱

# AND BEGIN AT MY SANCTUARY

In Ezekiel 9:1-6, God gave the prophet a vision:

> He cried … cause them that have charge over the city to draw near … Behold, six men came … every man with a destroying weapon in his hand …
>
> He called to the man clothed with linen, who had the writer's inkhorn at his side …and the Lord said to him …
>
> Go through the midst of the city and put a mark on the foreheads of those who sigh and cry over all the abominations that are done within it …

> To the others He said … Go after him through the city and … slay old and young … but do not come near anyone on whom is the mark; and begin at My sanctuary!

What is the difference between being slain or not? —Does your heart "sigh and cry" over abominations in your city?

In the praise song "Hosanna" there is a line:

> Break my heart for what breaks Yours; Everything I am for Your Kingdom's cause.

Do you think it breaks Jesus' heart to see these vulnerable children, made in God's image, being taught something contrary to His word. If it breaks Jesus' heart, shouldn't it break ours also?

Does your heart break for children experiencing loneliness and rejection in those emotional, preadolescent years being told by their teachers, school counselors and doctors that all their problems will be solved if they have their bodies mutilated with irreversible surgeries?

If you are silent, you are giving your consent to this treatment of children! Are you afraid of what people will say about you if you take a stand? You might possibly suffer some rejection.

British actor and podcaster Russell Brand stated in an Instagram reel:

> The central image of Christianity is an image of suffering. In the world of

positive thinking, well-being, there is a lot of self, self, self, on the shelf, shelf, shelf. Isn't it ... to make yourself happy and content ...

Isn't one of the great values of religion that we learn to use suffering to grow ... The type of Christianity that excites me is the idea that we can through surrendering ourselves become conduits for a Great Power ...

Our Lord and Savior Jesus Christ was pretty radical when it came to confrontations with power, a willingness to say things that are challenging. If, indeed, we are emulating Christ, isn't it somehow inherently political ... Is this the time ... to embrace our suffering as an opportunity to grow, to be willing to give up self-satisfaction in order to generate change. All the time in our content we are talking about change and politics and corruption and hypocrisy.

Is this (a cross) the perfect example we have been looking for and it has been right in front of our faces.

Keith Green wrote in the song, "Asleep in the Light," 1978:

Oh, bless me Lord, bless me Lord

You know, it's all I ever hear

No one aches, no one hurts

No one even sheds one tear

But He cries, He weeps, He bleeds
And He cares for your needs
And you just lay back
And keep soaking it in
Oh, can't you see it's such sin?
'Cause He brings people to your door
And you turn them away
As you smile and say
"God bless you, be at peace"
And all heaven just weeps
'Cause Jesus came to your door
You've left Him out on the streets
Open up, open up
And give yourself away
You see the need, you hear the cries
So how can you delay?
God's calling and you're the one
But like Jonah, you run
He's told you to speak
But you keep holding it in
Oh, can't you see it's such sin?

Maybe God is pushing the world toward a dividing moment, a decision-making time, a type of mini self-sorting out of the sheep and the goats.

# BRIDE OF CHRIST

Revelation 19:7–8:

> For the marriage of the Lamb is come,
> and his wife hath made herself ready. And
> to her it was granted to be arrayed in fine
> linen, clean and bright, for the fine linen
> is the righteous acts of the saints.

We are the Bride of Christ. Romance stories build up to a decision-making moment, a "forsaking of all others" and choosing "the one." Perhaps God is pushing the world to a decision-making moment, and some will choose the "all others." They will care so much about what others think about them that they will stay silent. They choose to be liked, friended, followed, trending, and invited to the parties.

John 12:42–43:

> ... but because of the Pharisees they did
> not confess Him, lest they should be put
> out of the synagogue; for they loved the
> praise of men more than the praise of God.

John 5:44:

> How can you believe, who receive
> honor from one another, and do not seek
> the honor that comes from the only God?

Others of us say, we no longer care about the "all others" all we care about is the one – Jesus!

Someone may say, I am not getting involved, but God knows my heart.

Yes, He does know your heart, and He knew Abraham's heart. Yet He still wanted to see Abraham be willing to take his son Isaac to the top of Mount Moriah. God intentionally put Abraham in a position of having to show on the outside what he really believed on the inside.

Imagine a husband watching football and you ask him, when was the last time you told your wife you love her; and he responds, I can't remember but she knows my heart.

You ask further, when was the last time you did anything to show your wife you love her, and he responds, I can't remember but she knows my heart. Then you tell him, I think it's about time we have a little talk about how marriage works!

People say, God knows my heart. Yes, He does, but He wants to hear some words out of your mouth and He wants to see some actions.

Deuteronomy 8:2:

> God led thee ... in the wilderness ...
> to prove thee, to know what was in thine
> heart, whether thou wouldest keep His
> commandments, or no.

Can love be love if it is not expressed, either in words or deeds? If you say you love someone, and they are in need, and you say or do nothing to help them, do you love them?

James 4:17:

> To him that knoweth to do good,
> and doeth it not, to him it is sin.

The church-at-large, with notable exceptions, has fallen down on the job of carrying out the great commission of making disciples of all nations. Now the church is put in the position of having to take a stand against evil.

God is giving us one last chance — if believers are so busy, consumed with their own lives and finding excuses why not to proclaim God's love, can they at least not be silent and give consent to evil?

If you are not going to do anything positive, at least don't be silent and give your approval to the negative. If you are not going to play a good offense, at least play a good defense.

When did being holy get twisted into giving consent to the unholy? Nominal Christians ignore Psalm 97:10, which says: "Let those who love the Lord hate evil."

One of the names for the Holy Spirit is *Paraclete* which means "Helper." In other words, you do not just pray and put your feet up on the couch. No, you pray and then do everything you can, and the Holy Spirit will help you!

Someone once said, there are three groups of people: Those who *make* things happen; those who *watch* things happen; and those who *wonder* what happened.

The early church prayed amidst persecution:

> Lord, behold their threatenings: and grant unto thy servants, that with all boldness they may speak thy word.

In Acts 18:9, Jesus appeared to Paul:

> Now the Lord spoke to Paul in the night by a vision, "Do not be afraid, but speak, and do not keep silent."

Paul wrote in 1 Corinthians 16:9, 13:

> For a great door, and effectual, has opened unto me, and there are many adversaries ... Watch ye, stand fast in the faith, quit you like men, be strong.

# WHAT IS YOUR STORY?

Someday you will be dead — but you will be in heaven because you believe that Jesus died on the cross to pay for all of your sins.

The line in the song "Amazing Grace" goes, "When we've been there ten thousand years, bright shining as the sun, we've no less days to sing God's praise, than when we've first begun!"

Imagine being in heaven ten thousand years,

walking on the streets of gold, and you get a chance to meet Moses. Maybe Moses will invite you over to his place. Jesus said, "In my Father's house are many mansions" (John 14:2).

Imagine you show up and there are others, David, Gideon, Elijah, Elisha, Deborah, Esther, the Apostle Paul, and more.

One by one, each tells their story of being on earth and facing great opposition, but trusting in God, they stood up with courage, and then God moved in a miraculous way.

Then everyone in the room will look at YOU and say—We haven't heard from you yet! Tell us your story! What are you going to say?

I would hate for Jesus to walk in the room, and a big screen come down and show great miracles and crowds coming to the Lord, and Him turning to you and saying — This is what I had planned for you to do when you were on Earth, but you just didn't have enough faith and courage.

You look back at your life, and see that big mountain that held you back only to find out it was just a tiny anthill – the fear of man. You can't go back to Earth to do anything else for the Lord, because you are already in heaven, because you believe that Jesus died on the cross to pay for all your sins!

Guess what? You are still on this Earth. You still have breath in your lungs. You still have feet that trod the soil. You still can do all those things that you will be known for forever!

The Lord chose for you to be alive on the Earth at this exact time. He knows every situation that is going on, and tells you:

> Fear not: for I have redeemed thee, I have called thee by thy name; thou art mine. (Isaiah 43:1)

> Fear not, nor be dismayed, be strong and of good courage. (Joshua 10:25)

> Fear not ... I am thy shield, and thy exceeding great reward. (Genesis 15:1)

God loves to wait until things look hopeless and then raise up little nobodies, who are small in their own eyes but big in faith and courage, to do great things! This is your turn!